Between Christ and the Black Man:
A Conversation on Race, Politics, and the Church in America

Also, available by Dr. Austin L. Scott on Amazon.com

For more, please visit our Youtube Channel,

"Destination Christlikeness" at:

https://www.youtube.com/channel/UC8PsqoTzY0FnMz9rp1r4OoQ

TABLE OF CONTENTS

Foreword

If, in all of our getting, our quest is to get "an understanding," then the book (*Between Christ and the Black Man*) is an excellent resource for Christians who not only believe in, trust, and lean upon God's word, but who also deeply desire to apply it practically in a very troubled world. It infuses Christian theology with a clear-eyed review of the history of African-Americans struggling to build our religious and educational institutions in the U.S. and within the African Diaspora. This book is, moreover, an excellent starting point for anyone who wishes to know Christ, His Gospel, the promise of salvation through Christ, and also the imperfect story of Christian church-building, and school-creation, "Black" and "White," in the United States. Framed deeply and richly in the American experience, this book consistently elevates Y'shua while confronting the problems of "race" and "racism" in the American experience. As any honest book rooted in the American experience must do, (*Between Christ and the Black Man*) highlights in great detail the nuanced, troubled, tragic and triumphant story of the Black community—"the Black man" and woman and child—in America.

The title of the book itself is instructive. Just as Richard Wright's classic poem *"Between the World and Me,"* and Ta-Nehisi Coates's recent book of the same name, underscores the horrors and tragedies of violence and threat directed at, and set upon, the Black body, mind, and spirit, so too does this book privilege the problem of white supremacy vis-a-vis the body, mind, and spirit of the African in America. This work also, however, significantly concerns itself with the "souls" of Black folk, and indeed the souls of all people. Genuinely evangelical, as opposed to "Dixievangelical," (*Between Christ and the Black Man*) rejects hatred, racism, and bigotry, making no excuses for them while at the same time running towards, not away from, conversion, controversy and paradoxes. From a survey of African spiritualism, religious and faith traditions, to a searing critique of white supremacist attempts to fit the square peg of African slavery into the round hole of purportedly Christian living, this book opens up powerful conversations and debates that are too often avoided, unknown, or simply swept under the rug.

Each chapter in this intriguing book reaffirms the fact that we are all, each of us, made in *"Imago Dei."* The Black man, woman and child are all made in the image of God, and not as an afterthought. White people, too, are made in the image of God, as are all the other peoples of the world. Nothing, then, should stand "Between Christ and the Black Man." Neither social construction nor man-made hatreds or injuries need block, or be allowed to wedge themselves between, God and any of His people. Like Paul, we can be persuaded that neither heights nor depths nor principalities nor thing present, nor past, nor any things of this world, or out of it, will separate us ever from the love of Christ Jesus. Thus, when Black worshipers are, in history, yanked from kneeling in prayer at segregated churches, as the book reminds us, the African response is in many ways more important than the white person's offense. See therefore the histories expounded in Chapter 1, *"In Response to White Nationalism: The Negro*

Church, HBCUs, and the Black Nation-State;" in short, liberation from white supremacy, Austin reminds us, rests largely in our own hands. Once you "got good religion, certainly Lord," then you know, unshakably, that you are a child of God. As such, you then must act like it. Get out from among them, if needed, but do what you must do to live in the fullness of God's promise, and particularly to embrace the superordinate charge of the Great Commission. Spreading the Gospel to all the corners of the earth would seem to require a fullness of confidence, a conviction that one is justified by faith, worthy of love, and worthy of a full life, one which rests upon and works itself from a center of love which is the Gospel of Christ.

Whilst readers, especially those of us of African descent, struggle to make sense of a troubled world, and a particularly painful yet paradoxically blessed and merciful past, its debates, contradictions, and conundrums, this book helps our understanding by exposing, in American and European history, disparate and troublesome approaches to Christian theology. Understanding others' people's misrepresentations and inversions, willful and not, can help us as we seek clarity and truth about not only who we are, but also who we are not. This book accordingly reminds us of reliable and unreliable catechisms, of old debates and philosophical as well as theological attempts, by others as well as by us, to make meaning of our unspeakably grievous wounds, of the Maafa or Transatlantic Slave Trade, and all that it has meant and continues to mean. Just as our Jewish brothers and sisters have often wondered "Where was G_d?" during the long night of the Holocaust, so—too—have "Blacks" throughout the Diaspora wondered aloud and silently about God's presence and seeming absence in our history, our lives, and our desperate pain. Faith, but a bold, defiant, resilient faith, nonetheless seems to endure for so very many of us, Jew and Gentile alike. A trust in God and a belief in His infinite wisdom endures. "We see through a glass dimly." Even so, our epistemological reach continues. In Chapter 5, "*In Search of An Identity: Black Religion, Philosophy, and Christ*" Austin especially helps us revisit, like Jacob wrestling the angel, the Black nation's philosophical and theological struggle with extracting meaning and purpose from our "weary years," "our silent tears," our times when "hopes unborn had died." In some way, the chapter picks up not only the arguments advanced by Black church leaders and missionaries, but also the very question that Martin L. King left us with: "Where do we go from here?"

As someone raised against the backdrop of the U.S. Civil Rights Movement, which—not for nothing—was led by "the Black church," I am naturally inspired by this book. After all, I have joyfully and fervently spent much of my life in the uniquely American institutions which this book privileges most: the Black church and the Black school. My first Black school was by birth; my last one was by choice. I grew up in Gary, Indiana at a time when "Lincoln Elementary" (our history is never very far behind us!) was almost entirely Black, to the tune of 99%. I received my Doctor of Ministry degree from an "HBCU" (or "Historically Black College/University), the Morehouse School of Religion, within the Interdenominational Theological Center, in Atlanta,

GA. In the vast gap of that time, I was blessed to study at three very different schools which were "PWIs" (or "Predominantly White Institutions"): a quite preppy DePauw University, the Ivy League's Columbia University, and, overseas, as a Rhodes Scholar (again, history never far behind!) at the University of Oxford. The rigorous study and teaching of political science, politics, and theology within or as a result of all these institutions has absolutely consumed and gratified me. Further, I have been called to the Ministry of Christ, and this is my greatest joy of all. At the current moment, I minister mostly in schools, where I encounter and do all I can to grow, inspire and guide thousands and thousands of young people, many of whom are future leaders. I also preach from the pulpit and wherever else God places me. I pray that my life is such a testament.

For all these reasons, I encourage you to curl up with this book. Mark it up, "talk back to the text:" ask, absorb, debate, expound, jot down questions, exclamation points, question marks, and "Amens." This book *(Between Christ and the Black Man)* is part of a very important daily conversation we must all have regarding our complex world, history, and the unique and similar calling which God has placed on all of our lives through His Son, Christ Jesus, Our Saviour, Light, Joy and Hope! In the final accounting, let there be nothing found creating distance between Christ and us.

~Pastor Carlton Long, D.Min.

In Response to White Nationalism:
The Negro Church, HBCUs and the Black Nation State

2020

Since the 17th century the idea of Black liberation in America has informed the dialogue concerning the political, social, economic, and spiritual direction that Blacks should take to move them from the concept of liberation to reality. Indeed, the very concept of liberation—from the introduction of the first African slaves to the teachings of the Bible—was developed, expounded, and propounded by the Black church. Inspired by their preachers, enslaved Africans in America believed that God would grant liberty either in this life or the next. Some believed in a mass exodus of slaves leaving their masters would transpire in much the same manner as the children of Israel departed from Egypt. Every aspect of their liberation was cloaked in Biblical language. Every route to freedom was "crossing the Jordan," and every liberator, a "Moses." Still, other Black Christian preachers concluded that the only path to freedom was through violence.

Nat Turner, for instance, fashioned himself to be a prophet of God and received what he believed were revelations from heaven of an apocalyptic battle between "black spirits" and "white spirits" (Gray 7-10). These visions culminated in Turner's famous revolt in Southampton, Virginia, costing him his life, the lives of his co-conspirators, and scores of his oppressors—including women and children (3-5). In the same way, Frederick Douglass, the famed abolitionist, writer, orator, and statesman, was an ordained minister and active member of the African Methodist Episcopal Zion Church in New Bedford, Massachusetts following his escape from slavery (Trotman 91). His faith in Christ was so deeply rooted that he described Christianity as ". . . the sigh of the soul for a noble; for herein is the true glory of God" (Dickerson 932). Yet, when referring to the opportunity for liberation that Blacks had during the Civil War by joining the army, this illustrious leader also urged that, "Who would be free themselves must strike the blow. . . fly to arms, and smite with death the power that would bury the government and your liberty in the same hopeless grave" (Douglass 3-4).

Given this American history, the following questions arise: why has liberation defined the Black experience in a country where

"White Christianity" was entrenched before the mass importation of African slaves to British North America in the early 1700s? What were the features of White Christian expression that compelled Blacks to establish independent Black churches prior to the Civil War and afterward? And why has the historic goal of "Black Christianity" been Black liberation from White Christianity in America? It is the position of this article that the reason for such discord, is White Christianity's centrality to the White nationalist agenda from the colonial era, while Black Christianity has always been tied to Black liberation from the White nationalist agenda.

White Christianity and The Origins of Racism in America

It is generally accepted that the first Africans to appear in colonial America in 1619 were indentured, most likely of West African origin, and thus likely descendants of a cultural belief in animism, spiritism, or Islam (Stevens 3; Hines et. al. 17; Raboteau 7). The presence of Islam was greatest in cities and most popular among the ruling and merchant classes (Hines et. al. 21). On the other hand,

West Africa's indigenous religions remained strongest in the forest region. They were polytheistic and animistic, recognizing a great number of divinities and spirits. Beneath an all-powerful, but remote, creator god were pantheons of lesser gods who represented the forces of nature. Other gods were associated with particular mountains, rivers, trees, and rocks. Indigenous West African religion, in other words, saw the force of God in all things. (21)

These deities were considered to be mystically tied to the ancestral dead, and were served by the head of the family or the oldest man in the family (Parrinder 136).

Despite possessing a heritage of ancient civilizations (e.g. the Ghanaian empire [circa 400 AD], Malian empire [1230-1460], and Songhai empire [1464-1591]), Africans were designated a permanently inferior class (Hines et al. 11-12, 57; Monroe 6). The relegation dishonored their past and sought to ensure a White harmonious present, one in which the White indentured servants might not rebel against the White planter class (Hines et al. 11-12,

57; Monroe 6). The British colonists not only seized upon this

stratagem but would later codify it into law. By the mid-1660s, the

Chesapeake colonies passed statutes that ". . . assumed servitude

was the natural condition of Black people" (Hines et al. 57).

Converting to Christianity could neither prevent Blacks from being

enslaved nor serve as grounds for their release (58). A 1729 issue

of the Boston Gazette is revelatory in this regard. In it, Philip

Yorke, Attorney General to the King of England, and Charles

Talbot, Solicitor General of England, offered the following opinion

on Black manumission through conversion in an advertisement,

stating,

> In Order to rectify a Mistake, that *Slaves become free, by their being in* England *or* Ireland *or being Baptized, it has been thought proper to consult the King's Attorney and Solicitor General in* England *thereupon, who have given the following Opinion, subscribed with their own Hands.*
>
> We are of Opinion, that a Slave, by coming from the *West Indies* to *Great Britain* or *Ireland*, either with or without his Master, doth not become free, and that his Master's Property, or Right in him, is not thereby determined or varied. And that Baptism doth not bestow Freedom on him, nor make any alteration in his temporal

> Condition in these Kingdoms. We are also of Opinion, that his Master may legally compel him to return again to the Plantations. (Glasson 279)

This opinion was in concert with the position of the Church of England, which lent spiritual authority to the government of England, and its control over the colonies. Being that the original thirteen colonies of what would become America were under British control, the Anglican Church, along with the Congregationalist Church, were the predominant Christian denominations of the pre-Revolutionary era.

Moreover, experiencing a lack of ministers and organizational infrastructure in the colonies, the Anglican Church found itself nearly powerless against the interests of the planter/master class that dominated the membership of the parishes (Clifton 38). Consequently, the Christian development of the enslaved Africans was entirely in the hands of their earthly masters who were opposed to their receiving any services or benefits from the church (38). During this period, Africans in British North America were minimally evangelized and even the idea of African-

American Christianity was rejected by their White Anglican counterparts (Stevens 7). It was not until 1702, when Rev. Dr. Thomas Brody founded the "Society for the Propagation of the Gospel in Foreign Parts among the Negroes in the Colonies," that this long period of stasis began to change. Claiming inspiration from the Holy Spirit, Brody secured a charter from King William III to found the organization and was thus sent by the Bishop of London to survey the condition of Anglicanism in the colonies (7). What he found was an overall spiritual decline (7). In response, ". . . [the] London organizers felt that missionaries as the evangelists of the Society should be utilized as a 'direct means to convert the heathen of all races whether Europeans, Indians, or Negroes'" (7).

However, what they accomplished in actuality was a retrenchment into the idea of inherent Black-Christian inferiority and White-Christian superiority. The gospel they preached did not include the equality of man, thus giving the planter/master the spiritual affirmation they needed to maintain a system which bound Blacks to a perpetual state of forced labor. Steven writes,

To gain success, the Society added some new teachings. The Society challenged the slaveholders to evangelize the slaves stating that a Christian slave was a better servant. Using Biblical passages, it emphasized that the slave should serve the slave holder as he/she was "found"; that the slave should serve the slave holder as serving God; and, that the hope of the slave is not in manumission, but it is in the future kingdom. (7)

This mind to subjugate Africans using socio-economic and spiritual means in colonial America was not an abstraction, but an outgrowth of the "British worldview" in the 17th century, one which asserted that in a racially stratified world where race was becoming more a description of a group's physical features than language and nationality, Britain was to be deemed at the top of the hierarchy (Jeremiah 86-87). This belief would be expanded into a program of colonization that would be exported globally and enhanced with each people group the British subdued, beginning with Ireland and Canada (Jeremiah 86; Rahman et. al. 15-17).

For example, after the British conquered the Irish elite at the Battle Boyne in 1690, they introduced the Penal Laws to Ireland in 1692 (Rahman et. al. 16-17). With the Anglican Church given the privileged position of spiritual authority, the Penal Laws ". . . comprehensively discriminated against Catholics who were prohibited from holding government office or commissions or entering the legal profession; this was coupled with acts that prevented them from owning land and limited their access to education and practice of their Catholic religion" (17). Simply put, the Penal Laws of 1692 ". . . secured a dominant relationship that allowed the Protestant community to force most Catholics outside the socio-economic and political system" (17). Therefore, being restricted from education and land ownership, the Irish (who were predominately Catholic) were reduced to the level of near-slaves—compelled to work the land for the English. The Indigenous, or First Nations, of Canada, did not fare any better. Justifying the European presence in Canada with the racist doctrine of "Terra Nullis"—the untrue and ahistorical claim that the lands of North

America were void of human life before Europeans arrived—the French and British fought fiercely over the land in the Seven Years' War (Alfred 45; Rahman 21). At the close of the war in 1763, the British gained control of French Canada and issued the Royal Proclamation, declaring sovereignty over the whole of North America (Rahman et. al. 21). Subsequently, the British engaged in ". . . the resource exploitation of indigenous lands . . . racism, expropriation of lands, and extinguishment of rights . . . [forcing the indigenous into a state of] wardship, and welfare dependency" (Alfred 43). These actions were given further legal sanction with the passage of the "Indian Act" of 1876. In addition to permitting the colonial government to continue its forceful confiscation of indigenous territories, it contained a framework of laws ". . . restricting the practice of their traditional cultures, languages, and religions, and undermining their institutions of self-government to assimilate the peoples so they [could] not sustain themselves as distinct cultures" (Rahman 22).

Moreover, despite the Society's concessions to the slave owners, converting enslaved Africans to Christianity was still an arduous task. It was understood by all that their conversion would not diminish racial hatred against them (Horne 66). To illustrate, when the Society opened its New York branch in 1704, a Frenchman named Elias Neu, joined the conversion cause (65). Engaging in door-to-door evangelism, the number of enslaved Africans he converted increased, but when some of the converts requested baptism, they were threatened with being sold to Virginia (66). Conversion aside, even free-born Black Christians were not safe from the reach of slavery in the colonies. Horne writes, "In 1709, Emmanuel Barselia, 'being a Spaniard,' complained that he was sold at Roanoke as a slave, this after being 'sold for a slave in New England,' though he was a 'Christian . . . born free'" (61).

As previously stated, it was the planter-class that comprised the vestry of the Anglican Church. Yet it was these members of whom one South Carolina minister in 1713 decried, ". . . the Masters of Slaves are generally of Opinion that a Slave grows worse by being a Christian; and therefore instead of instructing them in the principles of Christianity . . . malign and traduce those that attempt it" (Hines et. al. 66). The Anglican Church of the colonial era did little to dispel this opinion. For, although they demonstrated some concern about Black salvation,

> It [was] abundantly clear that the Church did not sponsor any cause or lead any effort on behalf of the manumission of the Negro. There is no evidence to indicate that any colonial Anglican minister or congregation in the period spoke out against the institution of slavery. The clergy did not condemn the master class for owning human slaves. In fact, they owned them themselves. In short, the Anglican Church remained indifferent to the abolition of slavery during the colonial era. (Clifton 52)

Given their position, it becomes apparent that while the Anglican clergymen would lambast the master class for their moral failure in withholding Christian education from their slaves, they took no issue with slavery itself, thereby offering Blacks a salvation that was intended to help them cope with, and even accept, their earthly

bondage. One prominent Anglican Bishop suggested that slave-

owning planters and ministers were themselves in bondage to the

"God of Gain" and were sincere "worshippers of Mammon" (52).

The Great Awakening and Racism

This salvation without manumission continued to be the

gospel preached from the early colonial era, into the first "Great

Awakening" from 1720 to the 1760s. The movement, which would

impact not only the church, but also the emerging American

government, and the family itself for generations, began when the

famed English preacher George Whitefield joined John Wesley in

his evangelistic outreaches on the streets of England (Quirion 2).

Whitefield would extend these efforts to America in 1740, and with

the help of revivalist Methodists, Baptists, and Scots-Irish

Presbyterians, create a permanent change in the religious fabric of

the nation (Quirion 2; Stevens 8). Part of what made this movement

so effective was Whitfield's preaching and extensive use of the

printing press to mass circulate his pamphlets. Such activity brought to America a revival of long-held Puritan beliefs that had been waning with the decline of American morality (Quirion 5; Lambert 13). The Puritans embraced the doctrine of Calvinism, which holds to the belief that God predestines all who are saved by His sovereign grace; the sacrifice of Christ was made only for those who are predestined, and the predestined are regenerated to choose God and can never lose their salvation (Quirion 3).

Within such a theological system is the teaching that these actions of God are the basis of a covenantal relationship between God and those whom He has predestined, and also between the predestined members themselves (3). Jerald C. Brauer, when explaining the Puritan interpretation of covenant in his work, "Religion and the Revolution" put it this way,

> A . . . thing to note about the covenant is its communal nature. Though it is grounded in the relationship between God and the individual, its purpose is not simply the salvation of individuals but rather the creation of a people. Individuals are not covenanted to God singly, in a lonely

relationship. Though the relationship between God and the soul is highly individual and subjective, it occurs only in the context of a community, the church. Churches are collections of individuals covenanted with each other to form a congregation of fellow believers. There is no true manifestation of the church apart from fellow believers owning a covenant with God and with each other.   (7-8)

These teachings of fellowship with God and of the need to practice Christian community swept British North America, and would become the foundational doctrines of American Protestantism (Quirion 2). Yet, despite the countless thousands of enslaved Africans who heard the gospel, converted, and were subsequently welcomed as "brothers" and "sisters" into the White Anglican, Baptist, Methodist, and Presbyterian evangelical churches, they nonetheless encountered in these same institutions the realities of racism and slavery. Hines et. al. describes their experience in these terms,

From the start, white churches seated black people apart from white people, belying claims to spiritual equality. Black members took communion *after* white members. Masters also tried to use religion to instill in their chattels such self-serving Christian virtues as meekness, humility, and obedience. (66)

Only Blacks who had their master's permission could attend the revival meetings, and those who did were either stationed in the balcony, outside, or given a separate sermon on how they should obey their masters (Lambert 12).

By taking such actions against Blacks in the church service, White Christians demonstrated that they were unwilling to enter a communal covenant with Christ that included Black people. Even after the Great Awakening of the 1760s, Africans continued to be a primary source of income for White churches in colonial America. One such church was Briery Presbyterian Church in Prince Edward County, Virginia, which maintained corporate ownership of slaves and hired them out yearly at auction for the entirety of their lives

(Oast 867). Presbyterian Minister William Hill, in his biography detailing his time pastoring the church, recalled how his salary was paid by these slave auctions (867). Hill considered a church owning slaves to be the ". . . worst kind of slavery" yet defended the institution as ". . . sanctioned by God as part of the natural hierarchical order of human domestic relations" (867-868). The financial rewards of slavery offset the need for members to tithe and helped fund the propagation of the Presbyterian faith (868). Consequently, because of the economic benefits of slavery, the church vested itself in the system regardless of its conflict with their doctrinal beliefs. It would not be until 1818 that the General Assembly of the Presbyterian Church would release even a nuanced statement condemning slavery (Moorhead 49).

It is evident, then, that the Great Awakening did not change the legal status of Blacks as chattel slaves and social inferiors to Whites. Instead, the stamp of these hierarchical relationships persisted in the White church through the Second Great Awakening to the close of the Civil Rights movement of the 1960s.

Nevertheless, despite the continued presence of racism and oppression during the Great Awakening, there was some good that resulted from the period. One secondary effect of the Great Awakening was that Blacks had come the closest to social equality with Whites than they ever had in colonial America. Many, while still enslaved, were being ordained as ministers in White churches and allowed to preach to White congregations (Hines et al. 66). The teachings of George Whitefield and Jonathan Edwards inspired Blacks in the North to advocate for equal rights in politics, education, and social relations (Stevens 8). In the South, evangelicals were opening doors for Blacks to become literate. For instance, Samuel Davies, a revivalist Presbyterian and contemporary of Whitefield promoted literacy for the slaves in Virginia because it helped them grasp the great tenets of faith (Lambert 14). In South Carolina, Hugh Bryan, a wealthy convert, provided such generous funding that ". . . Whitefield opened a school in Charleston to teach black children how to read" (Lambert 13). Entrepreneur William Bolton from Philadelphia, Pennsylvania, converted his dance hall to a school for Black children and was swiftly taken to court, where he prevailed (Lambert 13).

Despite these gains, Southern state legislators continued restricting Black participation in the church out of fear of insurrection, the religious undertones of the rebellions, and the disruption that the salvation of masters and slaves might bring to the Southern economy (May 237). "By 1850, every Southern state had enacted some restraint on the exercise of religion" led by South Carolina and Virginia, which enacted the ". . . first and most repressive religious assembly laws" (237). For example, in 1800 the South Carolina legislature expressly prohibited the religious activity of Blacks, stating, "It shall not be lawful for any number of slaves, free negroes, mulattos, or mestizos, *even in the company with white persons*, to meet together and assemble for the purpose of mental instruction or religious worship" (245). This law was later amended due to its unpopularity, to prevent ". . . slave patrols from dispersing any religious assembly in which the majority of attendants were white" (246). Black majority meetings could be broken up at any time with physical punishment inflicted, if necessary (246). This provision was intended to discourage unsupervised meetings that could foment insurrection. In 1804, the Virginia legislature enacted a statute which forbade ". . . nighttime religious meetings of slaves" (247). It was passed as part of the response to a foiled insurrection attempt made by an enslaved African named Gabriel and his co-conspirators near Richmond four years earlier (243-244). The 1804 law was revised in 1819 to include all nighttime meetings of slaves regardless of religion (247-248).

Racism, the Division of the Church, and the Civil War

These laws and their implementation in the White Protestant churches would cause division that anticipated the Civil War. Despite the different traditions of the churches, protestant evangelicalism was a unifying force in America (Goen 21). Yet, as a result of disputes over slavery, the Methodist, Baptist, and Presbyterian denominations—which enjoyed nationwide membership—were ". . . sundered into northern and southern factions long before political rupture, thus opening the first major cleavage between slaveholding and free states . . . to some extent [provoking] the crises of 1861" (21). The Presbyterian Church experienced two schisms, one in 1837 and another 1857 (21). The Methodist Episcopal Church divided in 1844, with the Baptists splitting the following year in 1845 (21). Relating the details of the national Baptist schism—and thereby shedding light on the source of the conflict in all the major denominations—Jeansonne writes,

> The chief objection of Southerners was that Northern anti-slavery advocates were trying to impose their sentiments on others. The North, which had nothing to gain, was pressing its views on the South, which had everything to lose. Southern churches withdrew, not to espouse pro-slavery doctrines, but to avoid further agitation on the subject. Slavery was not really an issue among Southern Baptists themselves. It was an established fact. The institution was not considered a theological or moral question. To Northern ministers the outlook was different. Living further from

slavery, they subjected it to a more critical scrutiny and

found it contradictory to such fundamental Christian

doctrines as the Golden Rule. The basic dispute, the

morality of slavery, was irreconcilable. (510)

Although the Northern Church appeared righteous in opposing

slavery, they were in reality exhibiting a hypocritical self-

righteousness. While they were against slavery, they were also

against social equality as the Southern Baptists were quick to point

out. Northerners wanted ". . . the South to free her slaves, but

would not give the freedmen jobs if they journeyed North" (511).

Southern Baptists wrote in the Memphis *Baptist Messenger* that

"Slavery . . . had originated in New England. New Englanders had

not decided that it was a sin until it had proved unprofitable there"

(511). In the majority of Northern cities, Blacks experienced

segregation in public transportation and accommodations (Tate

769). Northern White Christians were also not for spiritual equality

in the church, and it would be this attitude that precipitated the formation of the first Black denominational church in the United States in 1794.

One exception to the overall pattern of White churches embracing White nationalist ideology is the Quaker denomination, also known as, "The Society of Friends." Established in 1652 in England, by George Fox, the Quaker faith first appeared in Maryland in either 1655 or 1656 (Jordan 629). Their doctrine emphasized universal salvation, brotherhood, pacifism, and dependence upon the conscience (Sharpless 205; Hines et al. 93). Despite a history of involvement in slave trading and ownership, the Quakers were the first White group to call for abolishment (Hines et al. 93). As early as 1698, Quaker member Robert Pile, a prominent New-England civil-servant, released a paper urging his fellow Quakers to sever all ties with the slave-system per the teachings of Christ, stating,

> Sum time past theyr was sum inclination upon my mind to buy a negro, or negroes, by reason of my English servants being out of their times and having a great familie of small

children, might bee an help unto mee being for a tearm of life, that I and my children might have ye more liberty, &c; but theyr arose a question in mee, ye lawfulness theyr of under ye Gospel ministra- tion remembering the command of Christ Jesus, Do unto all men *as ye would have all man doe unto you; and wee would not will- ingly to be slaves tearm of life; also considering y^t Christ dieng for all mankind, they being a part, though yet ungathered.

(Cadbury 492)

This statement, coupled with the activism of Quakers Benjamin Lay (a former slave-holder), John Woolman, and Anthony Benezet, from the 1730s to the 1750s, culminated with the Society condemning slavery at its annual conference in 1758 (Hines et al. 93). The Quakers turned words into action. Hines et al. write, "Under Quaker leadership, anti-slavery societies came into existence in both the North and the Chesapeake. By 1774, such societies had joined African-Americans in petitioning northern legislatures and, in one instance, the Continental Congress to act against slavery or the slave trade" (94). Their support for Black liberation would involve rescuing kidnapped freedmen, investing in Black education, and alleviating Black poverty (Hamm et al. 7).

The Independent Black Church Movement

At the signing of the Constitution, there were no independent Black church organizations. Hence, ". . . all black churches were born in white congregations East, West, North, and South" (Walls 23). The beginnings of the independent Black church movement find their origins in the work of Andrew Byron and his brother Sampson (Raboteau 22). In the 1780s they started a fellowship near Savannah, Georgia, that by 1790, grew to nearly six-hundred congregants, and would become the First African Baptist Church (22). Two offshoots would arise from the church within the first decade of the 1800s (22). What made these churches unique is that despite the restrictions on their worship services they were able to operate independently. That is, they met without White supervision and could appoint their leaders without interference—a truly unique circumstance in the antebellum South

(22). But overall, between 1790 and 1820, against the backdrop of the Haitian Revolution and gradual abolitionism of the Northern states, ". . . black Episcopalians, Methodists, Baptists, and Presbyterians founded churches and struggled with church leaders to exercise varying degrees of independence from white control" even though they were regularly rebuffed (Raboteau 23; Polgar 229-231).

Notwithstanding these circumstances, the dependent status of Black Christians would begin to change in 1794 with the establishment of Bethel African Methodist Episcopal Church in Philadelphia, Pennsylvania—the first fully independent Black church in America. Founded by Richard Allen, who had been born a slave in 1760, and would later become a Methodist exhorter, the AME Church was established in response to specific acts of racial discrimination which occurred at St. George's Church in the early 1790s. Significantly, St. George's Church had been receiving considerable financial support from its Black parishioners for years

(Palmer 56; Raboteau 23). Allen's account of the seminal event is as follows,

A number of us usually attended St. George's Church on Fourth Street; and when the colored people began to get numerous in attending the church, they moved us from the wall, and on Sabbath morning we went to church and the sexton stood at the door and told us to go to the gallery. He told us to go and we would see where to sit. We expected to take the seats over the ones we formerly occupied below, not knowing any better. We took those seats. Meetings had begun, and they were nearly done singing, and just as we got to the seats, the elder said, 'Let us pray.' We had not been long on our knees, before I heard considerable scuffling and low talking. I raised my head up and saw one of the trustees H— M—, having hold of Rev. Absalom Jones, pulling him off his knees, and saying, "You must get up—you must not kneel here" . . . Mr. Jones said, "Wait until the prayer is over and I will get up and trouble you no more." With that he beckoned to one of the other trustees Mr. L— S—, to come to his assistance. He came and went to William White to pull him up. By this time prayer was over, and we all went out of the church in a body, and they were no more plagued with us in the church. (Palmer 56-57)

While the entire affair was unjust, it was merely another manifestation of the White nationalist spirit that had a near-ubiquitous presence in the denominational churches since the early colonial period. In response, the Black Christian membership separated themselves permanently.

Nevertheless, even after they separated and independently financed the construction of Bethel Church, White Methodists sought control of the institution. Raboteau writes, "The local Methodist ministers claimed ownership of property. When white Methodist ministers demanded control, Allen and his congregation refused and fought the case to the Pennsylvania Supreme Court, which decided in their favor (24). Other Black Methodist groups imitated Bethel Church of Philadelphia and established African

Methodist Churches in "Baltimore; Wilmington; Attleboro Pennsylvania; and Salem, New Jersey" (Palmer 57). These churches had similar experiences to Bethel in that they, too, were contending with White Methodists for autonomous control of their churches (Raboteau 24). As a result, these Black Methodists convened a conference at Bethel Church in 1816 to discuss such matters (24). What followed was the formation of the African Methodist Episcopal Church with Richard Allen elected its first Bishop (24). Other Black Methodist groups followed their example soon after. In 1815, the Union Church of Africans was founded in Wilmington, Delaware, and 1821 saw the formation of the African Methodist Episcopal "Zion" Church led by James Varick (Raboteau 24; Walls 23). Northern Blacks from other Christian denominations were also seeking to end White supervision of their churches. In 1794, St. Thomas African Episcopal Church was founded in Philadelphia; in 1804, an African Baptist Church was established in Boston; in 1805, the Jay Street Baptist Church was founded; the very first African Presbyterian Church was established in Philadelphia in 1807; in 1808 the Abyssinian Baptist

Church of New York was also formed, and in 1809 the First

African Baptist Church in Philadelphia was founded (Raboteau 24;

Palmer 59). "These black churches formed the institutional

structure for the development of free black communities"

(Raboteau 25). In other words, these churches were for all practical

purposes, the foundation of the Black nation-state.

The Negro Church as the Black Nation-State: Post-Revolutionary War Period

As is fitting for any state, the citizenry should rightly

assume that any policy put forward by the government would result

in the citizenry being the ultimate beneficiaries, for the citizenry of

the nation, is the nation. With Blacks from the colonial era to 1865

reduced to the level of beasts in the popular imagination—yet,

paradoxically counted as three-fifths of a person for federal

registration purposes in the U. S. Constitution (Hamilton et al. 302-

305)—Native Americans being denigrated as savages or non-

entities ("terra nullis"), and every other group in America deemed inferior, the only citizenry that remained were those who were White. As White people were the default citizenry, virtually all the benefits and control of the nation were in their hands. This pattern of racial consolidation of power is not unique. After all, Migdol, in his discussion on how ethnic solidarity was a pillar of nation-building for the newly formed states in the aftermath of the 20th century's two world wars—a similar context to that which preceded American independence—writes, "The state's self-preservation in the uncertain world . . . depended on selling to its people the notion that its political boundary was identical to the social boundary of the group—the nation—to which these people belonged and, thus, felt worth defending even at great sacrifice" (19). In this light, it can be deduced by the government's interactions with non-white peoples (especially Blacks) from 1619 to the present, that "America" is a White nationalist state, particularly since "Whiteness" has historically been the boundary outside of which the political, social, and economic benefits of policy do not cross. When policy did cross this boundary, it was only to pilfer resources from other groups so those within the boundary could have more to consume. This propensity explains, for example, the initial extension of British rule over North America, the doctrine of Manifest Destiny by the United States government, the expansion of slavery throughout the Americas, and the implementation of the Blacks Codes / Jim Crow legislation.

Bearing in mind these examples of government facilitated White supremacy, it is equally important to note how the permanent "White" citizenry came to be. Beginning in the late 1600s and early 1700s, what was already a British White-nationalist state in North America was increasingly becoming a Pan-European, White nationalist state. Following concerns over the Black to White population ratios tilting toward Blacks, a series of remedial events ensued, including: military conflicts, European migration, and the racial designation of "Whiteness" gradually expanding to include: the Irish and Scottish servant class; Protestants escaping persecution in France and Eastern Europe; European planters in the West Indies (particularly Jamaica and

Antigua) fleeing to the mainland from slave revolts; European Jewish migrants to Georgia; the Spanish who lost their East Florida colony to the British in 1763; and the French who ceded the Louisiana Territory to the U.S. government in 1803 (Horne 3, 44-45, 93, 26; Gallman 176; Theriault 297). These disparate people groups with unique cultures, civilizations, and conflicts dating back thousands of years would congeal into a generic "White" race. This racial classification would be put on the road to institutionalization when Congress passed the U.S. Naturalization Act in 1790. The law made it nearly effortless for Europeans (". . . any alien being a white person") to attain citizenship, the only requirement being residency in America for two years (Horne 249; Hines 114). Though the concept of Whiteness and those who qualify to be racially classified as "White," is subjective,

> To the scientific mind at the time the first statute was drafted, "white" meant Caucasian, as distinguished from Mongolian or yellow, Ethiopian or black, American or red, Malay or brown — following Blumenbach's classification

in 1781. Accordingly, naturalization [had] been denied

Chinese, Japanese, Burmese, Kanakas, and Canadian

Indians . . . No half-breed [was] a "white person" (HLR

561-562).

This population of Whites would counterbalance the equally

diverse, but genericized, "Black" slave population in America and

erect an echo chamber to reinforce the idea of White supremacy

consisting of political, social, economic, and spiritual forces

("spiritual" referring to the White Christian Church).

What is so striking about the development of the American

White nationalist construct is that despite the military conflicts

between the major colonial powers—Britain, France, Spain, and

the Netherlands— and despite the deepening rift between the

British Crown and her American subjects, and even still despite the

divisions in the White denominational churches over slavery, all

these discordant forces seemed to agree on one thing: the Black

man was of irredeemably inferior racial stock and had to be

confined to second-class status in every aspect of life. So powerful was this self-serving ideology, and the racial innovation of

Whiteness, that it would progress from being the policy of different

colonies controlled by different countries in North America,

survive the Revolutionary and Civil wars, and become the de facto

position of the United States government. This position was given

stark clarity by President Andrew Johnson in a letter he wrote to

Missouri governor, Thomas Fletcher, declaring, "This is a country

for white men, and by God, as long as I am President it shall be a

government for white men" (Trefousse 236). The powers of

government thus directed, there was no adequate national strategy

for the development of freed Blacks following the emancipation

events of the Revolutionary and Civil wars. In time, the Black

Church would come to assume this responsibility.

To illustrate, a year before the Peace of Paris was signed in

1783 by Britain and the U.S. to end the war,

> . . . Virginia had only 1,800 free people within a total black
>
> population of 220,582. By 1790 the state had 12,766 free
>
> people within a total black population of 306,193. By 1810

it was 30,570 within 423,088. . . . By 1830, four states

(Maryland, Virginia, New York, and Pennsylvania)

contained more than half of all free Blacks in America . . .

[But newly] freed black people . . . faced economic

difficulty, and their occupational status often declined.

Frequently they emerged from slavery without the

economic resources needed to become independent farmers,

shopkeepers, or tradespeople. In the North such economic

restraints sometimes forced them to remain with their

former masters long after formal emancipation. To make

matters worse, white artisans used legal and extralegal

means to protect themselves from black competition so

African Americans who had learned trades as slaves had

difficulty employing their skills in freedom. (Hines et al.

96; Harris 605)

To address these challenges, Blacks developed mutual-aid societies

and voluntary associations that would be complementary to the

work of the church.

To illustrate, the first recorded voluntary association formed by free Blacks was the African Union Society of Newport, Rhode Island in 1780 (Harris 609). This organization emphasized moral living among Blacks and was involved in nearly every aspect of Black life—helping with ". . . recording their births, deaths, marriages, and by seeking to apprentice black youth in useful trades" (609). As a further expression of their benevolence, the society did not restrict these services to its members, but extended them to all Black people in Newport (609). Interestingly, the African Union Society spearheaded an early emigration movement to Sierra Leone, a settlement established in 1787 by the British for African loyalists in the Revolutionary War (610). There were numerous organizations such as the aforementioned. In the North, for instance, they included in part: the Free African Society (established in 1787 by Richard Allen and Absalom Jones); the Brown Fellowship Society (1790); the Female Benevolent Society of St. Thomas (1793); the Benevolent Daughters (1796); the African Benevolent Society (1808); the New York African Society for Mutual Relief (1808); the American Female Bond Benevolent

Society (1817); and in 1818 the Female Benezet (Hines et al. 114).

Southern free Blacks also established mutual aid societies in the

"upper South" region of Washington D.C., Richmond, Virginia,

and Charleston, South Carolina which comprised of the Burying

Ground Society (1815); the Beneficial Society (1815); the Resolute

Beneficial Society (1818); the Christian Benevolent Society

(1839); the Humane Brotherhood (1843); and in 1844, the Unity

and Friendship Society (Harris 617).

These institutions—mostly the creation of the Black

Church—were the primary drivers of spiritual, political, social, and

economic uplift of the Black community in the post-Revolutionary

War period. They provided, ". . . sickness and disability benefits,

pensions for deceased members' families, burial insurance, funeral

direction, cemetery plots, credit unions, charity, education, moral

guidance and discussion forums"—all the functions of a nation-

state (614). These organizations also demanded Christian character

and moral rectitude of their members as a rebuke to the prevailing racist ideology that Blacks needed slavery to control their ". . . laziness, ignorance, and immorality" (Raboteau 26). So serious were they to maintain respectability that members were expelled for disreputable behavior (Harris 616). The churches were also hotbeds of political activism, hosting forums, and organizing for emancipation. Walls writes, "In the days of slavery the Zion ministers were generally leaders of the anti-slavery movement and their pulpits were always open to anti-slavery lectures. If no other house could be obtained for an anti-slavery meeting it was known that a Zion church could be had. The doors of this church were never closed against one who wanted to plead for the oppressed" (23).

Education for free Blacks and their children was also a problem. For instance, in Philadelphia, taxpayer-funded schools were virtually non-existent until 1818 (Kammerer 300). Once they became available to the public, Blacks were not allowed to attend them until 1822, when the schools would be segregated (300). The lack of access to public education between 1776 and 1822 compelled Blacks to find funding for private education (300). Yet,

even when funding for private education was provided by anti-

slavery societies and other benevolent groups, Black children

would often not be able to attend, as they were an indispensable

source of family income (300). Blacks would face similar problems

in other cities throughout the North. Case in point, in the 1840's,

Black Bostonian integrationists and separatists were in a heated,

and sometimes violent, dispute over whether to integrate Black

children into the White schools or maintain the tax-supported

Black schools (Hancock 115-119). At the center of the conflict was

the all-Black, Smith School (Hancock 115-119). The separatists

won in a decision given by the Boston School Committee's

majority report in 1846. Hancock writes,

> [T]he School Committee emphatically stated that color or
>
> complexion was "not the ground of distinction" for
>
> determining whether a child was to go to a black or white
>
> school. The boundary was established and maintained on
>
> the grounds of "races, not colors" . . . . the majority report

argued that "amalgamation is degradation" for both races since it threatened the "genuine virtues" peculiar to each race. The report concluded by emphasizing the white committee's racial conception, describing students "colored children, or the descendants of the African race" whose unique educational needs due to their race—needs the committee outlined as an inferior ability to use "faculties of invention, comparison, and reasoning"—mandated separate schools. (119)

With seeming foresight into these events, in 1796, shortly after the founding of Bethel AME Church, Richard Allen and the board of trustees opened a day school for children (called "The First Day School") and a night school for adults (Kammerer 309). The school met in the church building and provided basic religious education and literacy to some sixty students (309). Eventually, by the 1850s, Bethel's education program or "Sabbath School" would expand to include, ". . . 350 children, two superintendents, and 25 teachers,

11 males, 14 females," making it ". . . a center for black religious education in Philadelphia" (310).

In St. Louis, arguably the city most open to Black education in the antebellum period, the responsibility for educating the Black population was mostly assumed by the Black Church. These churches provided instruction in Christian doctrine, reading, writing, and trades (Bellamy 149). One great proponent of Black education in Missouri was ex-slave John Berry Meachum. After obtaining his freedom and relocating to St. Louis in 1815, he was ordained in 1826 and became pastor of the First African Baptist Church in 1827 (149). He espoused industrial education, self-help, and racial solidarity, but not abolition through violence, surmising that this approach would bring needless suffering to Blacks (150). Instead, he favored purchasing the freedom of as many Blacks as possible until the entire system would be abolished (150). The other Black churches in St. Louis were just as bold about the education of Blacks. Bellamy writes,

By 1860, there were five black churches in St. Louis, and all of them had educational programs. Schools under the guise of Sunday Schools for religious instruction, were conducted in the basement of all of St. Louis' black churches. They charged a tuition fee of $1.00 per month for those who could afford to pay, although no one, not even a slave, was turned away if he could not meet the financial obligation.

These schools were conducted under a guise in response to an 1847 Missouri law that made it illegal to educate Blacks in the state. Thus, during the post-revolutionary period, through the formation of independent Black churches, Blacks began to forge their destiny as a nation within a nation. All of their efforts were a counter to the White nationalist juggernaut that was the U.S government, which sustained itself from the revenues of Black enslavement. Notwithstanding the oppression, under the drumbeats of Civil War in the 1850s, to the initiation of the conflict in 1861, and the subsequent Reconstruction Era of the late 1800s, Black churches would elevate their education programs out of their basements and begin to house them in colleges and universities—ushering in a new phase of Black self-determination and nationhood.

Historically Black Colleges and Universities (HBCUs) as the Black Nation-State

The direct path from slavery to freedom is education (Douglass, "Narrative" 34). Education allows one to understand, negotiate, shape, and ultimately transform his or her reality. Chattel slavery necessitated that this creative power be crushed out of Black men and women in order for them to fully accept a systematized process of dehumanization, one that combined corrupted Biblical interpretation, White supremacist indoctrination, and near ubiquitous legal protection for slavery by the United States government. Thus, the slave system instilled in Blacks a sense of hopelessness as they were being psychologically and emotionally transformed from human beings into beasts of burden. This agenda was clearly articulated by Representative Henry Berry in a speech he delivered in the Virginia House of Burgesses in 1832. Referring to the "Black race," he declared,

> Sir, we have, as far as possible closed every avenue by which light might enter their minds; we have only to go one step further—to extinguish the capacity to see the light, and our work would be completed; they would then be reduced to the level of the beasts of the field, and we should be safe; and I am not certain that we would not do it, if we could find the necessary process—and that under the plea of necessity. (3)

The light Berry is referring to is the light of education, and it is largely because of their 250-year banishment from this light by the slave system that Blacks were so tenacious in seeking to acquire this instrument of liberation. They attended secret classes at night, tricked the children of their White masters into teaching them the alphabet, attended Sunday Schools that doubled as literacy programs, and seized upon countless other opportunities to learn—however they were afforded—at great personal risk. Indeed, it is because of this dogged persistence that from 1619 to 1850, under withering White nationalist oppression, twenty-nine Black Americans would overcome all odds to earn their Bachelor's degrees (Humphries 57). By 1870, merely five years after the abolition of slavery by the Thirteenth Amendment, Blacks would contribute 1 million dollars to educate their people (Hines et al. 298).

Following the Civil War, which, in American history was a second emancipation event, the realization that basic literacy, industrial training, and Christian education were needed for the nearly four-million newly freed Blacks would mark the next phase in the evolution of the Black nation-state. With financing from Black churches, Northern philanthropists, and missionary societies, HBCUs would prepare Blacks to assume a more secure and respectable place in the broader American economy in the postbellum era. The first of these institutions had their advent before the Civil War, namely, Lincoln University in 1854 and Wilberforce University in 1857—established by the AME Church

(Humphries 57). Black colleges would begin as ". . . social settlements . . . where freedmen . . . began the process of assimilating into a civic order defined by Anglo-Protestant culture as free laborers and citizens" (Allen et al. 266). These freedmen and their descendants—comprising the majority of the student population at HBCUs—were mostly poor and illiterate (268). In the face of such a diversity of academic need, these colleges not only offered college-level curricula, but also elementary education, secondary education, and college preparatory coursework (268). In a repudiation of the slave system, HBCUs would welcome all who were eager to learn. Allen et al. write,

> HBCUs were the first southern institutions to open their doors to everyone; they did not discriminate and accepted students from any gender, race, creed, or color . . . Therefore, along with the Black students that largely dominated HBCU campuses, these institutions often educated the children of the White missionaries who helped establish these institutions, Native Americans, poor Whites,

and international students from Asia, Africa, Latin America, and the Caribbean. White female and Jewish students also enrolled in the professional programs offered by some HBCUs . . . (268)

Gradually, these institutions would become cultural, political, and intellectual hubs in the global Black liberation struggle. W. E. B. Du Bois, widely regarded as a premier leader of pan-Africanism, was a pillar of Black education at Fisk University; and in 1901, world-renowned educator, Booker T. Washington, sent three graduates from the Tuskegee Institute to Togo to assist the populous with improving their cotton production (Zimmerman 1362). Booker T. Washington had significant influence on the African continent as,

> Black leaders in several African countries embraced his work for its emphasis on self-help and racial solidarity. They admired Tuskegee Institute as a model of black achievement without necessarily subscribing to its curriculum. Perhaps his most noteworthy follower on the

continent was John Lagalabalele Dube, the

Congregationalist minister and graduate of Oberlin College

who visited Tuskegee in 1899 and embraced the gospel of

industrial education. Often called the "Booker T.

Washington of South Africa," Dube returned to Natal and

in 1901 built the Zulu Christian Industrial School. He

established the Bantu Business League, modeled on

Washington's National Negro Business League. . . . He

became the founder of the African National Congress, the

organization that eventually brought the downfall of the

apartheid system. (Norrell 201)

African presidents Kwame Nkrumah of Ghana, Nnamadi Azikiwe

of Nigeria, and Kamuzu Banda of Malawi were also educated by

HBCUs (Parker 738; Oguntoyinbo).

On the other hand, one of the early challenges HBCUs

faced was deciding on an educational philosophy that best suited

the needs of their constituents. Black colleges would have to decide

whether their curricula should emphasize vocational skills, liberal arts, or both—a debate that persists to the present. This early debate would foreshadow the more comprehensive philosophical dialogue between Booker T. Washington and W. E. B. Du Bois in the late nineteenth and early twentieth centuries. Booker T. Washington—a former slave, Hamptonian, educator, and founder of the Tuskegee Institute—maintained that the brutal industrial training Blacks received during slavery could, in freedom, be applied to laying an economic foundation for Blacks to accumulate the wealth needed for future pursuits in liberal arts (Washington 21-22). Du Bois, a Harvard man, on the contrary, believed that Black manhood and labor were void without a broad understanding of the world and the place Blacks occupy within it (Du Bois 33). He further believed that an elite minority consisting of the best of those who would receive a liberal education should lead the Black masses towards a higher political, social, cultural, and economic status (33-34). On the whole, HBCUs would integrate elements of both philosophies into their curricula.

Furthermore, HBCUs are credited with being ". . . singlehandedly the driving force to establishing the Black middle-class" (Exhano 70). Exhano further writes, that by 1970, "HBCUs had graduated at the undergraduate level 75% of all Black American PhDs, 75% of all Black army officers, 80% of all Black federal judges, and 85% of all Black doctors" (71). This trend continued and increased in the early 2000s with HBCUs graduating, "80% of Black officers in the United States military, 80% of Black federal judges, 63% of Black physicians, 60% of Black attorneys, and 50% of Black teachers and engineers" (Abelman & Dalessandro 106). After the 2017-2018 academic year, HBCUs conferred a cumulative 48,300 associate's, bachelor's, master's, and doctoral degrees, with Blacks earning ". . . 43 percent of the 5,500 associate's degrees, 81 percent of the 32,600 bachelor's degrees, 71 percent of the 7,700 master's degrees, and 62 percent of the 2,500 doctor's degrees" (Fast Facts). Such a broad academic impact of HBCUs on the national economy is preceded by their economic impact locally, as HBCUs stimulate every local and regional economy where they are located. A report

by the United Negro College Fund in 2014 found that "HBCUs

generate 14.8 billion in *total* economic impact for their local and

regional economies. . . . 134,090 jobs for their local and regional

economies. . . . " and $130 billion in lifetime earnings for their

graduates (HBCUs Make America).

Conclusions

The concepts of "nation" and "state" generally refer to a

group's collective identity and how they relate to the government

they choose to live under and have to organize their lives

(Grotenhuis 28). A nation is more of an ideological construct that

pertains to a group's self-concept, while a state is identified by the

institutions that facilitate the laws, mores, and norms that arise

from that nation's self-concept (28). According to the 1933

Montevideo Convention on the Rights and Duties of States, "The

State as a person of international law should possess the following

qualifications: a) a permanent population; b) a defined territory; c)

government; and d) capacity to enter into relations with other states" (Grotenhuis 25). The state also exists to perform five primary functions,

1. Creating space for participation in political decision making so that the polity becomes inclusive and open for citizens;

2. Providing security for people against outside and inside aggressors and criminals;

3. Providing justice so that people are treated as equals, fairly and without discrimination;

4. Providing basic social services that enable people to live their lives in dignity;

5. Creating an infrastructure to facilitate economic life and making rules to let economic life be fair. (Grutenhuis 25-26)

Given the functional, rather than the territorial definition of a state, it is evident that the Black Church, and all the early mutual aid societies, voluntary associations, schools, colleges, and auxiliary institutions it established or influenced throughout American history, constitutes a Black "nation-state" in America.

Concerning identity and self-conceptualization, the Black Nation-State is essentially a mashup of a multitude of West and Central African tribal groups with their respective languages, cultures, and styles of governance. Without their consent, and with no thought as to how they would interact, these disparate groups were forged by the fires of slavery into one non-descript ethnicity—the "Negro." This burden of slavery laid upon the nation by White nationalist avarice denied Blacks their humanity. Thus, Blacks, before the end of the Civil War, had not the opportunity to craft an all-encompassing identity except that they were men and women, not animals. Their primary occupation was survival. Yet, out of their determination to survive, the necessary elements for developing a national identity arose. For in their suffering, they turned to Christ and embraced the promises of freedom, justice, and equality found in both the Bible and the Constitution. Around these transcendent beacons, Blacks built a state, comprising churches, primary schools, colleges, voluntary associations, and mutual aid societies under the direction of Christian leaders and denominational councils.

Marginalized by racism, these institutions served as platforms for political activism, safe havens for Black expression, safety nets for the hard-pressed, engines of economic growth, and allies to all persecuted groups. That Blacks could accomplish such feats in the face of unrelenting hatred across a span of four hundred years is miraculous. Yet, while these achievements are worthy of the highest honors, they are also worthy of lamentation. For, if Blacks could accomplish so much, so quickly, with scant resources, and negligible local, state, and federal support from the pre-Revolutionary era to the close of the Civil Rights movement in the 1960s, it begs the questions, "What more could have been achieved if White nationalism were not an ever-present obstruction to their progress? How much further could America have advanced spiritually, politically, socially, and economically if the Black

Nation-State were allowed to contribute freely to the general welfare?"

Unfortunately, racism in America can be compared to a cake that has finished baking, and is thus in a state that none of its ingredients can be removed. The only way to have a different cake is to bake a new one. Similarly, racial hatred as a cake of customs was baked into the fundamental essence of American society. Therefore, racism can never be extricated from the country without the entire structure collapsing. America's only hope, it seems, is a new civilization, established by a new humanity, one that upholds love and selflessness as its highest ideals. This "new creation" can only come through Christ and His Church—the cornerstone of the Black Nation-State.

References

Abelman, Robert, and Amy Dalessandro. "The Institutional Vision of Historically Black Colleges and Universities." *Journal of Black Studies*, vol. 40, no. 2, 2009, pp. 105–134. *JSTOR*, www.jstor.org/stable/40282625.

"Aliens. Naturalization. 'Free White Persons.'" *Harvard Law Review*, vol. 23, no. 7, 1910, pp. 561–562. *JSTOR*, www.jstor.org/stable/1325297.

Allen, Walter R., et al. "Historically Black Colleges and Universities: Honoring the Past, Engaging the Present, Touching the Future." *The Journal of Negro Education*, vol. 76, no. 3, 2007, pp. 263–280. *JSTOR*, www.jstor.org/stable/40034570.

Bellamy, Donnie D. "The Education of Blacks in Missouri Prior to 1861." *The Journal of Negro History*, vol. 59, no. 2, 1974, pp. 143–157. *JSTOR*, www.jstor.org/stable/2717326.

Berry, Henry. *The Speech of Henry Berry (of Jefferson) in the House of Delegates of Virginia, on the Abolition of Slavery,*

Internet Archive, 1832, p. 3, *Open Library,*
https://openlibrary.org/books/OL6526329M/The_speech_of_Hen
ry_Berry

Brauer, Jeral C. *Religion and the American Revolution.* Fortress
Press, 1976, pp. 7-8

Cadbury, Henry J. "An Early Quaker Anti-Slavery Statement." *The
Journal of Negro History,* vol. 22, no. 4, 1937, pp. 488–
493. *JSTOR,* www.jstor.org/stable/2714238.

Clifton, Denzil T. "Anglicanism and Negro Slavery in Colonial
America." *Historical Magazine of the Protestant Episcopal
Church,* vol. 39, no. 1, 1970, pp. 29–70. *JSTOR,*
www.jstor.org/stable/42973244.

Coupet, J. "Strings attached? linking historically black colleges and
universities public revenue sources with
efficiency." *Journal of Higher Education Policy and
Management, 39*(1), 2017, pp. 40-57.
doi:10.1080/1360080X.2016.1254427

Dickerson, Dennis C. "Frederick Douglass: America's Prophet."

Church History, vol. 87, no. 3, 2018, p. 932 *EBSCOhost*,

doi:10.1017/S0009640718002160.

Douglass, Frederick. "Men of Color, To Arms." *Library of*

Congress, 1863, pp. 3-4, www.loc.gov/item/mfd.22005.

Douglass, Frederick. *Narrative of the life of Frederick Douglass,*

an American slave. Boston: Anti-Slavery Office, 1849, p.

34, *Library of Congress*, www.loc.gov/item/82225385.

Du Bois, W. E. B. "The Talented Tenth" *The Negro Problem*,

edited by Booker T. Washington, 1903, pp. 33-34.

University of Minnesota

moses.law.umn.edu/darrow/documents/Talented_Tenth.pdf.

Gallman, Nancy O. "Reconstituting Power in an American

Borderland: Political Change in Colonial East Florida." *The*

Florida Historical Quarterly, vol. 94, no. 2, 2015, pp. 169–

191, *JSTOR*, www.jstor.org/stable/24769177.

Gerald, Alfred T. "Colonialism and State

Dependency." *International Journal of Aboriginal Health*,

vol. 5, no. 2, 2009, pp. 43-45.

jps.library.utoronto.ca/index.php/ijih/article/view/28982

Glasson, Travis. "'Baptism Doth Not Bestow Freedom':
Missionary Anglicanism, Slavery, And the Yorke-Talbot
Opinion, 1701-30." *The William and Mary Quarterly*, vol.
67, no. 2, 2010, pp. 279–318. *JSTOR*,
www.jstor.org/stable/10.5309/willmaryquar.67.2.279.

Goen, C. C. "Broken Churches, Broken Nation: Regional Religion
and North-South Alienation in Antebellum
America." *Church History*, vol. 52, no. 1, 1983, pp. 21–
35. *JSTOR*, www.jstor.org/stable/3167066.

Gray, Thomas R. and Turner, Nat, *The Confessions of Nat Turner*.
Zea E-Books in American Studies. no.11, 1831, pp. 1-10.
digitalcommons.unl.edu/zeaamericanstudies/11.

Grotenhuis, R. "Nation and State." *Nation-Building as Necessary
Effort in Fragile States*, by *Amsterdam University Press*,
2016, pp. 25–44. *JSTOR*,
www.jstor.org/stable/j.ctt1gr7d8r.5.

Hamilton, Alexander, et al. "The Federalist." *The Great Books of the Western World*, Robert P. Gwinn, 1990, pp. 29-258. *Encyclopedia Britannica.*

Hamm, Thomas D., et al. "'A Great and Good People' Midwestern Quakers and the Struggle Against Slavery." Indiana Magazine of History, vol. 100, no. 1, 2004, p. 3. EBSCOhost, search.ebscohost.com/login.aspx?

Hancock, Scott. "The Elusive Boundaries of Blackness: Identity Formation in Antebellum Boston." *The Journal of Negro History*, vol. 84, no. 2, 1999, pp. 115–129. *JSTOR*, www.jstor.org/stable/2649042.

Harris, Robert L. "Early Black Benevolent Societies, 1780-1830." *The Massachusetts Review*, vol. 20, no. 3, 1979, pp. 603–625. *JSTOR*, www.jstor.org/stable/25088988.

Hine, Darlene Clark, et al. *The African-American Odyssey*. Third edition, Pearson Education, 2006, pp. 17-21, A-9.

Horne, Gerald. *The Counterrevolution of 1776: Slave Resistance
and the Origins of the United States of America*. MJF
Books, 2014 pp. 66

Humphries, Frederick S. "A Short History of Blacks in Higher
Education." *The Journal of Blacks in Higher Education*, no.
6, 1994, pp. 57–57. *JSTOR*, www.jstor.org/stable/2962465..

Jeansonne, Glen. "Southern Baptist Attitudes Toward Slavery,
1845-1861." *The Georgia Historical Quarterly*, vol. 55, no.
4, 1971, pp. 510–522. *JSTOR*,
www.jstor.org/stable/40579712.

Jordan, David W. "'Gods Candle' within Government: Quakers
and Politics in Early Maryland." *The William and Mary
Quarterly*, vol. 39, no. 4, 1982, pp. 628–654. *JSTOR*,
www.jstor.org/stable/1919006.

Kammerer, Elise. "Uplift in Schools and the Church: Abolitionist
Approaches to Free Black Education in Early National
Philadelphia." *Historical Social Research / Historische*

Sozialforschung, vol. 42, no. 1 (159), 2017, pp. 299–

319. *JSTOR*, www.jstor.org/stable/44176034.

Lambert, Frank. "'I Saw the Book Talk': Slave Readings of the

First Great Awakening." *The Journal of African American*

History, vol. 87, 2002, pp. 12–25. *JSTOR*,

www.jstor.org/stable/1562488.

Monroe, J. Cameron. "Power and Agency in Precolonial African

States." *Annual Review of Anthropology*, vol. 42, 2013, pp.

17–35, *JSTOR*, www.jstor.org/stable/43049288.

Moorhead, James H. "Between Hope and Fear: Presbyterians and

the 1818 Statement on Slavery." *The Journal of*

Presbyterian History (1997-), vol. 96, no. 2, 2018, pp. 48–

61. *JSTOR*, www.jstor.org/stable/26751306.

May, Nicholas. "Holy Rebellion: Religious Assembly Laws in

Antebellum South Carolina and Virginia." *The American*

Journal of Legal History, vol. 49, no. 3, 2007, pp. 237–

256. *JSTOR*, www.jstor.org/stable/25664424.

Migdal, Joel S. "State Building and the Non-Nation-State." *Journal of International Affairs*, vol. 58, no. 1, 2004, pp. 17–46. *JSTOR*, www.jstor.org/stable/24357934.

National Center for Education Statistics. *Fast Facts: Historically Black Colleges and Universities*. nces.ed.gov/fastfacts/display.asp?id=667#:~:text=Black%20students%20earned%2043%20percent,by%20HBCUs%20in%202017%E2%80%9318, 2018.

Norrell, Robert. *Up from History: The Life of Booker T. Washington*. First Harvard University Press, 2011, p. 201.

Oast, Jennifer. "'The Worst Kind of Slavery': Slave-Owning Presbyterian Churches in Prince Edward County, Virginia." *The Journal of Southern History*, vol. 76, no. 4, 2010, pp. 867–900. *JSTOR*, www.jstor.org/stable/27919282.

Oguntoyinbo, Lekan. "HBCUs Produce Leaders Not Only Domestically, But Also Abroad." *Diverse: Issues in Higher*

Education, 25 Feb. 2013,

diverseeducation.com/article/51530/

Palmer, Edward N. "The Origin of Independent Negro

Denominations." *Negro History Bulletin*, vol. 9, no. 3,

1945, pp. 55–62. *JSTOR*, www.jstor.org/stable/44174494.

Parrinder, E. G. "Islam and West African Indigenous

Religion." *Numen*, vol. 6, no. 2, 1959, pp. 130–141. *JSTOR*,

www.jstor.org/stable/3269310.

Parker, Jason C. "'Made-in-America Revolutions'? The 'Black

University' and the American Role in the Decolonization of

the Black Atlantic." *The Journal of American History*, vol.

96, no. 3, 2009, pp. 727–750. *JSTOR*,

www.jstor.org/stable/25622476.

Polgar, Paul J. "'To Raise Them to an Equal Participation': Early

National Abolitionism, Gradual Emancipation, and the

Promise of African American Citizenship." *Journal of the*

Early Republic, vol. 31, no. 2, 2011, pp. 229–258. *JSTOR*,

www.jstor.org/stable/41261611.

Quirion, Kory R.T. "The First Great Awakening: Revival and the

Birth of a Nation," *Bound Away: The Liberty Journal of

History*, vol. 1, no. 2,

digitalcommons.liberty.edu/ljh/vol1/iss2/3.

Raboteau, Albert J., *Canaan Land: A Religious History of African-

Americans*. OUP, 2001, pp. 7-25.

Rahman, Aziz, Mary Anne Clarke, and Sean Byrne. "The Art of

Breaking People Down: The British Colonial Model in

Ireland and Canada." *Peace Research* 49, no. 2, 2017, pp.

15-38,143-144,

search.proquest.com/docview/2236675592?accountid=35812.

Sharpless, Isaac. "Presbyterian and Quaker in Colonial

Pennsylvania." *Journal of the Presbyterian Historical

Society* (1901-1930), vol. 3, no. 5, 1906, pp. 201–218.

JSTOR, www.jstor.org/stable/23322501.

Sidwell, Mark. "George Liele: Missions Pioneer." *Profiles of

African-American Missionaries*, edited by Robert J. Stevens

and Brian Johnson, William Carey Library 2012, p. 9-12.

Stevens, Robert J., "Christianity and the Slave [1600s]." *Profiles of African-American Missionaries*, edited by Robert J. Stevens and Brian Johnson, William Carey Library 2012, p. 3.

Tate, Gayle T. "Free Black Resistance in the Antebellum Era, 1830 to 1860." *Journal of Black Studies*, vol. 28, no. 6, 1998, pp. 764–782. *JSTOR*, www.jstor.org/stable/2784816.

The Editors at Encyclopedia Britannica. "Hastings Kamuzu Banda." *Encyclopedia Britannica*, 2020, www.britannica.com/biography/Hastings-Kamuzu-Banda.

Theriault, Sean M. "Party Politics during the Louisiana Purchase." *Social Science History*, vol. 30, no. 2, 2006, pp. 293–324. *JSTOR*, www.jstor.org/stable/40267908.

Travis Glasson. "'Baptism Doth Not Bestow Freedom': Missionary Anglicanism, Slavery, And the Yorke-Talbot Opinion, 1701-30." *The William and Mary Quarterly*, vol. 67, no. 2, 2010, pp. 279–318. *JSTOR*, www.jstor.org/stable/10.5309/willmaryquar.67.2.279.

Trefousse, Hans L. *Andrew Johnson: A Biography*. W.W. Norton

and Company, 1997, p. 236.

Trotman, C. James. "Frederick Douglass's

Spirituality." *Counterpoints*, vol. 406, 2012, pp. 89–

103. *JSTOR*, www.jstor.org/stable/42981621.

United Negro College Fund. HBCUs Make America Strong: The

Positive Economic Impact of The Nation's Historically

Black Colleges and Universities. 2014, p. 5.

cdn.uncf.org/wpcontent/uploads/HBCU_Consumer_Brochu

re_FINAL_APPROVED.pdf?_ga=2.149479038.91765347.

1592886535-5369459.1592886535

Walls, William J. "AME and AMEZ History." Profiles of African-

American Missionaries, edited by Robert J. Stevens and

Brian Johnson, William Carey Library 2012, p. 23.

Washington, Booker T. The Future of the American Negro. 1899,

pp. 21-22, University of Macau,

library.um.edu.mo/ebooks/b17839063.pdf

Zimmerman, Andrew. "A German Alabama in Africa: The

Tuskegee Expedition to German Togo and the

Transnational Origins of West African Cotton Growers."

The American Historical Review, vol. 110, no. 5, 2005, pp.

1362–1398. JSTOR,

www.jstor.org/stable/10.1086/ahr.110.5.1362

A Hand Up for the Black Community: HBCUs and the Work College Model

2019

In the United States, there are 103 federally recognized historically Black colleges and universities located in 19 southern and border states (Brown, 2013). Historically Black Colleges and Universities were established as a means of social uplift and Christian indoctrination for African-Americans freed from slavery by the Civil War (Coupet, 2017). Financed by northern philanthropists and missionary societies, most HBCUs—with exception of Lincoln University and Wilberforce University—were founded during the reconstruction era of the nineteenth century (Cantey, Bland, Mack & Davis, 2013). Their objective was to train Black teachers to provide four million African-American children and adults in the South an adequate primary and secondary education (Cantey et al., 2013). These colleges provided training in ministerial work, vocations, and other practical skills in agreement with the objective of the Freedmen's Bureau to prepare African-Americans or wage labor (Cantey et al., 2013).

However, as the southern United States was still dependent upon Black labor at the close of the Civil War, Blacks were subjected—often violently—to slave-wage agricultural jobs

(Coupet, 2017). Thus, the financial support of southern states for

Black education was all but abandoned, leaving the survival of

these newly formed HBCUs in the care of the Freedmen's Bureau

(Coupet, 2017). This trend of underfunding and defunding Black

education by southern states will continue into the present. The

Hatcher Act of 1887 directed federal funds to be equally distributed

by states to higher education institutions (Black and White) for the

purpose of developing agricultural and mechanical science

programs—which most HBCUs emphasized—unless they deemed

otherwise (The Hatch Act 1887, 2017; Coupet, 2017). But southern

states funded white institutions at significantly higher levels

(Coupet, 2017).

Additionally, the Merrill Act of 1862, also known as the

Land Grant College Act, provided federal funding for states to

appropriate land to build colleges with a concentration in

agriculture, education, and military sciences (Brown, 2013). The

supplement to this bill, the Merrill Act of 1890, required the funding expenditure to be inclusive of institutions enrolling African-Americans (Brown, 2013). This clause led to the formation of 17 public land-grant HBCUs from 1890 to 1912 (Esters & Strayhorn, 2013). Yet, with a segregated economy dependent upon Black farming, the public training schools southern and border states created for Blacks were training students below a high school level (Coupet, 2017). They further opposed any liberal arts training that would challenge racism and kept the institutions underfunded (Coupet, 2017). The 1965 Higher Education Act also provided funding for HBCUs but did not address the states' inclinations towards inequitable funding, nor did it address the need for racial inclusiveness (Coupet, 2017; Glater, 2016).

Presently, though HBCUs receive funding from grants, tuition, corporate gifts, and private donations, they are still heavily reliant upon Pell Grants, aid grants, scholarships, veteran's benefits, work-study aid, social security benefits of dependent children, and federal loans (Cantey et al., 2013). All these revenue sources are dependent on the local, state, and federal government, and the economic conditions of the time (Cantey et al., 2013). This

uncertain form of funding creates the potential for budget deficits,

faculty and staff layoffs, decreased student enrollment, and even

school closure (Cantey et al., 2013). Federal and state funding

constitute 75% of all financial support received by public HBCUs

(Jones, 2016). Moreover, as private gifts make up only a small

amount of institutional funds, the average public HBCU

endowment in 2009 was close to $49,000,000, half the national

average of all public colleges and universities at $87,000,000

(Jones, 2016). Compounding this disparity is the reality of

continued spending cuts by state governments. In 2008, public

HBCUs in Alabama, Louisiana, Mississippi, and North Carolina

enrolled a larger number of African-Americans than predominately

White institutions (PWIs) but only received a fraction of the

funding (Jones, 2016). In fact, public HBCUs in the states

previously mentioned received a larger portion of spending cuts

that were made from 2007-2012 (Jones, 2016). For instance, during

this period, Louisiana State University (a PWI) experienced a 25%

reduction in state appropriations, while HBCUs Southern University and A&M College, and Grambling State University received decreases of 45% and 36% (Jones, 2016).

As the survival of HBCUs appears to be threatened by a lack of political will to adequately fund their institutions and difficulty raising non-public capital, it may be necessary for them to consider a third option for operating: the Work College model. Established by Congress in 1992 (Kim, 2018), the Work College applies to those post-secondary education institutions which have had a comprehensive work/service/learning program in operation for at least two years (Work College, 2018). In this model, students work either on campus to meet the school's operational needs, or with corporate partners of the college in the surrounding areas to pay their tuition (The Work College Consortium, About, 2018; Paul Quinn College, 2014). There are numerous benefits to this model for students and institutions. For example, Paul Quinn College in Dallas, TX became the first Historically Black College or University to earn this designation and graduate students with less than $10,000 in student loan debt (The Work College

Consortium, Paul Quinn, 2018). Alice Lloyd College, another

work-higher education institution, charges no out-of-pocket costs

for students in its 108-county service area, which includes parts of

Kentucky, Ohio, Virginia, West Virginia, and Tennessee (The

Work College Consortium, Alice Lloyd, 2018). The college also

does not accept any direct local, state, or federal government funds,

and has no long-term debt (The Work College Consortium, Alice

Lloyd, 2018). With these benefits, how can the Work College

model help more HBCUs become less financially independent on

government funding for operating expenses?

Curiously, there is scarce research on the Work College

model outside of the works of think-tanks and associations.

However, what these sources offer is instructive. The Work

College was first validated by Congress in Title IV of the Higher

Education Act of 1965, which designated funding for schools

pursuing that educational approach (Bolger & Collins, 2018).

Continuing their support of the policy, Congress, as recently as the fiscal year 2017-2018 dispersed $8,390,000 to colleges belonging to the Work College Consortium (Bolger & Collins, 2018). Institutions belonging to this group must meet four requirements to access these exclusive funds: 1) the Work College model must be fully integrated into the curriculum, policies, and practices of the school, 2) students must fully engage in the work program their entire college careers, 3) instruments for evaluating student work performance must have equal rigor to those which measure their academic performance, and devise goals for student improvement, and 4) supervisors of student workers must receive professional development training (Bolger & Collins, 2018).

Moreover, Pickford (2018) documents how the Work Colleges are distinct from the traditional four-year institutions in that students who attend these colleges pay greatly reduced tuition or no tuition at all. These students traditionally represent the most underprivileged and underrepresented groups in America (Bidwell, 2018). But they are offered this opportunity in exchange for their participation in the school's comprehensive work program in which they work in a job function or community service for up to 20 hours (Pickford, 2018). For instance, at Alice Lloyd College, student job assignments are based on a blue collar to white collar continuum as they matriculate through college (Rudibaugh, 2015). The student labor supports the mission and basic staffing needs of the Work College, which can include buildings and grounds maintenance, food services, and administrative tasks, minimizing operating costs (Pickford, 2018; Bolger & Collins, 2018).

In 2017, for example, student labor at Paul Quinn College amounted to the equivalent of 15 full-time employees each semester (Pickford, 2018). Student workers are also evaluated regarding their performance on their work assignments, receiving a type of work transcript to complement their academic transcript (Bidwell, 2018). When students are lacking in their skills in an area, the work supervisors collaborate with instructors to practice the skill in class (Bidwell, 2018). As a result, in the most recent Work Colleges Consortium survey, 68% of Work College graduates indicated that their undergraduate training better prepared them for the workforce, compared with 53% and 47% of their private and public-school peers (Pickford, 2018). Despite the numerous benefits of the Work-College, federal funds cover less than half of the operating expenditures of the schools, causing many to supplement the federal support with revenue from endowments and private gifts (Pickford, 2018). Work Colleges must match their grant funding dollar-for-dollar without exception (United States Department of Education, 2017). Federal Work-Study funding can be transferred to the Work College allocation up to 100%, but these funds must also be matched dollar-for-dollar and used exclusively to reinforce the "self-help-through work element of the program" (United States Department of Education, 2017).

Conclusion

Understanding the Work College model and how it can be adopted by HBCUs is worthy of further exploration. It is evident from the stressors of uncertain state and federal funding, and the inability to raise enough private capital, that HBCUs must find an alternative means of operating to remain solvent. It is my supposition that the Work College model is that alternative, as it emphasizes efficiency, financial discipline, and the integration of the student body into the school workforce. Continuing the same course of traditional governance will only further jeopardize already vulnerable HBCUs. For instance, in 2012, Virginia State University was sanctioned by the Southern Association of Colleges and Schools (SACS) for failure to comply with financial standards and St. Paul's College had its accreditation revoked after 124 years of operation (Crawford, 2017).

In 2012, four other schools including Edward Waters, Jarvis Christian College, Fort Valley State University, and Savannah State University were placed on cautionary status (Crawford, 2017). Fisk University in 2013 was also at risk of being closed (Crawford, 2017). In 2014, Norfolk State University was placed on probation by SACS (Crawford, 2017). In 2016, four HBCU presidents were terminated due in part to accreditation and financial problems (Crawford, 2017). Notwithstanding these woes, there is hope. Seven HBCUs in 2012 had their accreditations extended for 10 years, and two were removed from "warning" status (Crawford, 2017). The Work College model has the potential to move HBCUs from hope to sustainability.

References

Bidwell, A. (2018). *Is the Work College Model the 'Wave of the Future' for Reaching Underserved Students?* Retrieved from National Association of Student Financial Aid Administrators' website: https://www.nasfaa.org/news-item/15082/Is_the_Work_College_Model_the_Wave_of_the_Future_for_Reaching_Underserved_Students

Brown, C. M., II. (2013). The declining significance of historically black colleges and universities: Relevance, reputation, and reality in obamamerica. *The Journal of Negro Education, 82*(1), 3-19. doi:10.7709/jnegroeducation.82.1.0003

Coupet, J. (2017). Strings attached? linking historically black colleges and universities public revenue sources with efficiency. *Journal of Higher Education Policy and Management, 39*(1), 40-57. doi:10.1080/1360080X.2016.1254427

Cantey, N. I., Bland, R., Mack L. R., & Joy-Davis, D. (2013).

Historically black colleges and universities: Sustaining a

culture of excellence in the twenty-first century. *Journal of*

African American Studies, 17(2), 142-153.

doi:10.1007/s12111-011-9191-0

Crawford, J., II., (2017). HBCUs: Accreditation, governance and

survival challenges in an ever-increasing competition for

funding and students. *Journal of Research Initiatives*, 2(3).

Retrieved from

https://digitalcommons.uncfsu.edu/jri/vol2/iss3/1/?utm_sou

rce=digitalcommons.uncfsu.edu%2Fjri%2Fvol2%2Fiss3%2

F1&utm_medium=PDF&utm_campaign=PDFCoverPages

Esters, L. L., & Strayhorn, T. L. (2013). Demystifying the

contributions of public land-grant historically black

colleges and universities: Voices of HBCU presidents. *The*

Negro Educational Review, 64(1-4), 119-135. Retrieved

from http://gateway.proquest.com/openurl?url_ver=Z39.88-

2004&res_dat=xri:bsc:&rft_dat=xri:bsc:rec:iibp:00443592

Glater, J. D. (2016). Debt, merit, and equity in higher education

access. *Law and Contemporary Problems, 79*(3), 89-113.

Hatch Act of 1887. (2017). Hatch Act of 1887, 1. Retrieved from

https://search.ebscohost.com/login.aspx?direct=true&db=ap

h&AN=21213126&site=ehost-live

Kim, A. (2018). *Innovating Out of Student Debt*. Retrieved from

the Progressive Policy Institute's website:

https://www.progressivepolicy.org/publications/policy-

memo/innovating-out-of-student-debt/

Paul Quinn College. (2014). *Work Program*. Retrieved from

http://www.pqc.edu/nation-building/work-program/

Rudibaugh, L. M. (2015). *Helping the way we are needed:

Ethnography of an Appalachian work college* Available

from Publicly Available Content Database. Retrieved

from https://search.proquest.com/docview/1696750479

The Work Colleges Consortium. (2018). *About Work Colleges*.

Retrieved from http://www.workcolleges.org/about-work-

colleges

The Work Colleges Consortium. (2018). *Member Colleges*.

Retrieved from

https://www.workcolleges.org/colleges/paul-quinn-college

The Work Colleges Consortium. (2018). *Member Colleges*.

Retrieved from

https://www.workcolleges.org/colleges/alice-lloyd-college

United States Department of Education. (2017). *Federal Student*

Aid Handbook. Retrieved from

https://ifap.ed.gov/ifap/byAwardYear.jsp?type=fsahandboo

k&awardyear=2018-2019

Work Colleges Program, 34 C.F.R. § 675.41 (2018). Retrieved

from https://www.ecfr.gov/cgi-

bin/retrieveECFR?gp=&SID=ae6bb11592a71907de9d2ee0

117a1e0a&mc=true&n=pt34.3.675&r=PART&ty=HTML

Returning Home:

Economic Cooperation Between African-Americans and Africa

2016

Since the decolonization of Africa and the civil rights movement of the 1950's and 60's, both Africans and American Americans have made significant economic strides. Following the passage of the Civil Rights Act of 1964, 4.5 million African-Americans earned a college degree; and 100,000 obtained doctoral degrees (Worde, 2013). Between 2002 and 2007, Black owned business increased 60.5%, totaling 1.9 million—a generation of 137.5 billion in receipts (US Census Bureau, 2008). In Africa, from 1960 and 2000, the gross domestic product increased by 60% (Ndulu & O'Connell, 2010). Both groups have prospered from economic activities intra-regionally, intra-continently, and intercontinentally (Adriamanajara, 2015; World Trade Organization, 2015), but have not been deliberate about forging bilateral economic partnerships.

Numerous African-American business owners cite infrastructure, high internet usage fees, and access to capital as hindrances to conducting business in Africa (Spiropolous, 2014) Yet, with one trillion dollars in economic power (Weeks, 2013),

African-Americans are a fitting choice for Africa to consider as a long-term mutually beneficial partnership. Although the overall African-American community has one trillion dollars in spending power, this research will analyze only the top ten wealthiest African-American owned businesses, their industries, and how they would make natural partners in the economic development of Africa. Since six out of the ten companies operate in two common industries, their potential impact will be calculated collectively instead of independently.

According to Black Enterprise Research (2013), the top ten wealthiest African-American owned businesses are as follows in table 1,

Rank	Company	Industry	Revenue (in Millions)
1	Worldwide Technology Inc.	IT Products	$6,400.000
2	Act-1 Group	Staffing Services	$2,254.480
3	Bridgewater Interiors LLC.	Auto Parts Supplier	$1,500.000

4	Modular Assembly Innovations LLC	Auto Parts Manuf. and Assembly	$1,919.802
5	Manna Inc.	Quick Service Restaurants	$630.000
6	The Anderson-Dubose Cos.	Food and Paper Distribution	$545.701
7	Global Automotive Alliance LLC	Automotive Parts Supplier	$520.000
8	Thompson Hospitality	Food and Facilities Management	$485.000
9	Radio One Inc.	Radio One Broadcasting	$448.000
10	SET Enterprises Inc.	Metal Processing	$390.000

World Wide Technology Inc.

With over $6,400,000,000 in revenue, Worldwide Technology Inc. is by far the largest African-American owned business (B.E. Research, 2014). Founded in 1990 by CEO David L. Steward, the company is a leading IT products and services provider with a specialization in systems integration and supply chain solutions (Smith, 2006). These include,

. . . advanced technology center to design, build, educate, demonstrate, and display technology products and integrated architectural solutions; big data, collaboration, and data center; enterprise networking solutions that focus on enterprise campus and branch, data center networking, high-end routing and optical, enterprise mobility, and software defined networking; and security solutions that focus on big date security analytics, advanced persistent threat defense, breach readiness, enterprise secure mobility, secure cloud and data center, and secure networking. (Bloomberg Business 2016, para. 1)

With such expertise, Worldwide Technology Inc. could be an indispensable tool in addressing the unemployment and IT infrastructure need in Africa.

For example, in North Africa, the youth unemployment rate is 30% for males and 45% for female youth (International Labor Organization, 2016). In Africa south of the Sahara Desert, "informal employment"-defined as work in low-skilled jobs with insufficient opportunities for training; low wages, long hours, and no social protections (International Labor Organization, 2016)-accounts for 60%-80% of all employment, and 90% of new jobs (Benjamin & Mbaye, 2014). In lieu of this, African governments have responded by taking steps to create a more digital economy in their countries. Rwanda merged the Youth and IT ministries between 2012-2013 (Institute for Development Studies, 2016). Egypt, Ghana, Kenya, Morocco, Nigeria, and South Africa have since 2013 become stakeholders in The Rockerfeller Foundation's Digital Jobs Africa Initiative, which seeks to,

> . . . [I]mpact the lives of 1 million people in the [aforementioned] six countries by catalyzing sustainable Information and Communications Technology enabled employment opportunities for African youth who would not otherwise have the opportunity for sustainable growth . . . (The Rockerfeller Foundation, 2013, para. 1)

> With forty major locations around the world, including: United States, Japan, The Netherlands, Brazil, Singapore, China,

Hong Kong, Mexico, and the United Kingdom, World Wide Technology Inc, (WWT Inc.) has no presence in Africa (World Wide Technology Inc., 2016). An approach to become involved in Africa is for WWT Inc. to join the Digital Jobs Africa Initiative as a stakeholder. Then they could open an office in a stabilized country such as Rwanda (Gallup, 2015); and sign memoranda of understanding with the six nations in the initiative to provide technical support in their critical need areas to realize specific targets. By WWT Inc. filling the technological void in the six nations, they could also provide training to youth participants in the initiative on how to equip, install, utilize, maintain, and sell their products to the emerging industries in their countries. This will provide the youth with training and employment, and WWT Inc. with a significant foothold on the African continent.

Act 1 Group

Founded in 1978 by Janice Bryant Howroyd, Act 1 Group is located in Terrance, California, and offers,

. . . permanent placement and temporary staffing services from more than 70 branch locations in the U. S. The company provides administrative, professional, and light industrial personnel for companies in the entertainment, medical, and financial services, telecommunications, and manufacturing sectors, among others. Its technical and professional services unit supplies contract IT and engineering professionals. Other affiliated offer . . . services including background screening, print purchasing, document scanning, distance learning, workforce training, and a travel agency. (Dun and Bradstreet 2016, para. 1)

Having annual sales of nearly $300 million (Dun and Bradstreet, 2016), Act 1 Group would be an effective partner in the development of Africa, particularly for the south African nation of Botswana.

As a market economy, Botswana is rated Africa's least corrupt country; with a "One Stop Shop" model for entrepreneurs to open businesses, a corporate tax rate of 22%, and is ranked 30th globally for economic freedom (Heritage, 2016). Act 1 Group would be a suitable candidate to provide workforce training and staffing solutions to employers throughout the country. In 2006, the government of Botswana released its 10th National Development Plan, outlining the country's vision and mission for the following ten years after publication (Modise & Mosweunyane, 2014). According to the plan, the Botswana government concluded that in order to address the mismatches and shortages of professionals in certain fields—especially in Information and Communications Technology—their education policy would concentrate on producing not only competencies and skills that meet international standards, but also on providing preparatory training for the workplace environment. They specified that,

> . . . [Y]outh will be provided with life skills. Graduate employment and internship programs will be instituted to provide exposure to the work environment, inculcate good work ethics and provide opportunities for career development. In recognition of the need to align skills with

opportunities in the economy, youth will be supported to develop competencies and match their talents with opportunities . . . (World Health Organization 2009, pg. 101)

As the largest Black-owned staffing agency, with expertise in workforce development and training for employability, Act 1 could assist the Botswana government with achieving the goal of providing youth with graduate internships, and overall job readiness training. In the public sector, they could begin by selling employment services to the Diamond industry, which is the main driver of economic growth in Botswana (World Bank, 2015). Due to the incongruity between labor supply and demand, and increasing unemployment (Modise & Mosweunyane, 2014), Act-1 could help serve as intermediary between employment and labor. This could be accomplished by Act-1 Group collaborating with colleges and universities in the country—especially the University of Botswana—to produce curriculum to future graduates, delivering workforce development and job readiness skills. In the private sector, Act 1 Group could provide assistance by obtaining accreditation as a workforce development and job readiness training institution from the Botswana Training Authority. The Botswana Training Authority has accredited ". . . a total of 264 institutions that were made up of 113 private, 55 consultancies, 14 public, and 10 nongovernmental organizations" (Modise & Mosweunyane, 2014 pg. 304). Act-1 Group could thus become a full-service consultancy, since it has expertise in every major industry.

Bridgewater Interiors LLC

Established as a joint-venture between Epsilon Technologies LLC, and Johnson Controls Inc. in 1998, Bridgewater Interiors LLC specializes in manufacturing and assembly of complete automotive seating systems, overheard systems, and center consoles (Bridgewater Interiors LLC 2011). They provide their services to General Motors, Ford, Chrysler, and Honda (Bridgewater Interiors LLC, 2011).

Modular Assembly Innovations

Hailed as the top minority-owned business of 2015 in Central Ohio by Columbia Business First (Newpoff, 2015); Modular Assembly Innovations is the parent corporation of certified minority companies, offering manufacturing and assembly solutions in East Liberty, Ohio; Lincoln, Alabama; and Greensburg, Indiana (Ohio Manufacturer's Association, 2013).

Global Automotive Alliance

According to Crane's Detroit Business: "Fast 50: Fastest Growing Companies" (2015), Global Automotive Alliance LLC ranked 20th in revenue growth between the year 2011 and 2014; growing from $329 million to $539 million. Global Automotive Alliance LLC is an automotive manufacturer, assembler, warehouse sequencer, and is involved in warehouse logistics.

Bridgewater Interiors LLC, Modular Assembly Innovations, and Global Automotive Alliance LLC combined are worth over $3 Billion, and comprise the backbone of African-American business representation in the automotive industry in the

United States; making their expertise invaluable for the rising automotive industry in Africa. According to PriceWaterCooper's 2014 report: "Africa's Next Automotive Hub," Nigeria is slated to become the epicenter of automotive manufacturing in Africa. With an estimated population of over 177 million (Central Intelligence Agency, 2014) and a growing middle class of over 40 million (Corral, Molini & Oseni, 2015), there is a significant opportunity for long-term investment and growth.

Having imported approximately $4 Billion worth of vehicles in 2012 alone, and with two-thirds of those vehicles being certified pre-owned; the annual demand for vehicles in Nigeria is close to half a million—100,000 new, and 400,000 used (National Automotive Council, 2014). Nigeria is now seeking to turn that demand into a sustained market for the auto industry by manufacturing vehicles locally (National Automotive Council 2014 & PriceWaterCooper, 2014). In 2013, the Nigerian government granted licenses to 35 companies to assemble vehicles in the country which included: Kia, Hyundai, Nissan, Ford, and TaTa

(PriceWaterCooper, 2014). Through this effort, and with continued government support, the Nigerian auto-industry is on track to produce over 6 million vehicles using locally secured components by 2050 (PriceWaterCooper, 2014). Bridgewater Interiors LLC, Modular Assembly Innovations, and Global Automotive Alliance LLC as original equipment manufacturers, could expand their services into the Nigerian market—opening plants and warehouses that would supply the car brands that were previously operating in the country.

Manna Inc.

Employing 2,180 full-time staff, Manna Inc. is the largest minority owned business in Louisville, KY (Stines, 2016). Founded in 1996 by Ulysses "Junior" Bridgeman, the company exists as an owner-operator of 160 Wendy's restaurants in five states, and 103 Chili's restaurants in seven states (Stines, 2016 & Edmond Jr., 2011).

The Anderson Dubose Cos.

The Anderson-Dubose Company is a logistics and a food and non-food distribution provider to more than 500 McDonald's and Chipotle's in Ohio, Pennsylvania, New York, and West Virginia (Anderson Dubose Cos., 2013). The company was established in 1991 by Warren Anderson and Stephen Dubose who purchased a McDonald's distributorship from the company Martin Brower (Anderson-Dubose Cos., 2016).

Thompson Hospitality

Thompson Hospitality is a contract food service provider to government institutions, businesses, and Historically Black Colleges and Universities (Dun & Bradstreet, 2016). Thompson Hospitality operates in 45 states and four countries, and was formed through a partnership with food service provider, The Compass Group, in 2005 (Thompson Hospitality, 2015 & 2016).

Combined, the aforementioned food service industry companies with over 1.5 billion in annual revenue, functioning as one entity, would represent the largest Black-owned full-service food provider, distributor, and restaurant operator on Earth (BE Research, 2013). Their integrated capacity and experience would make them a valuable asset in providing employment opportunities in the food service industry in Africa. When a company deliberates whether or not enter a new market, they evaluate, among other criterion, the development of the population, the development of gross domestic product, the development of gross domestic product per capita, the conditions for repatriation, the conditions for sales, the operational risks, the political system, and the political risks (Grunig & Morschett, 2012). Accounting for these factors, Mauritius, a small island nation of the African continent, is a seemly destination for investment and partnership.

Concerning governance, Mauritius up to 2014 was ranked in first place by the Mo Ibrahim Index for African governance five years in a row (Kalumiya & Kannon, 2015). Equally impressive, is that the 2016 Index of Economic Freedom ranks Mauritius in first place regionally and 15th globally for economic freedom (Heritage, 2016). The country also has a vibrant food and accommodations sector with restaurants helping to contribute 18.8% of gross

domestic product in 2014 (Kalumiya & Kannon, 2015). For

Manna Inc, The Anderson-Dubose Cos., and Thompson Hospitality

to enter the Mauritian food service market, they could consider the

opportunities presented by the tourism industry in the country.

Tourism contributed 25.5% of GDP ($2.8 billion) in 2014, and is

forecasted to rise by 24.5% of GDP by 2025 (World Travel and

Tourism Council, 2015). With this in mind, if the three companies

consolidated around the Chili's franchise operated by Manna Inc.,

they could successfully participate in the $2.8 billion industry,

promoting employment in and economic development in the

country.

Chili's has locations in 32 countries worldwide (Chili's,

2016). Of those 32 locations, 18 are in countries that send

approximately 351, 647 people as tourists to Mauritius on an

annual basis (Statistics Mauritius, 2015). With international name

recognition, and a fun and energetic atmosphere, using TV's and

Ziosk tablets for entertainment and convenience (Brinker

International, 2014); "Manna Inc. Consolidated" would make a strong competitor in the food service market. According Juwaheer, Pudaruth, and Ramadin (2013) in a study which surveyed 600 respondents from 23 shopping malls on 33 mall attributes that influence the shopping experience in Mauritius; the factor which had the greatest impact on the overall willingness to visit the shopping malls of Mauritius was the "entertainment facilities and events" (p. 185). Using this impetus, "Manna Inc. Consolidated" could find placement in the country by partnering with the management of its 17 main shopping centers; (Mauritius Attractions, 2016). They could begin with Bagatelle, the largest shopping mall in the country near the capital city of Port Louis (Mauritius Attractions, 2016).

Radio One

Based in Silver Springs, Maryland, Radio One is the largest broadcaster to the African-American community in the United States (Dun and Bradstreet 2016). The company operates through four divisions: Radio Broadcasting, Reach Media, internet, and cable television (Yahoo! Finance, 2009). The company's assets include 55 stations in 15 primarily urban markets located in Atlanta, Baltimore, Charlotte, Cincinnati, Cleveland, Columbus, Dallas, Detroit, Houston, Indianapolis, Philadelphia, Raleigh-Durham, Richmond, St. Louis, and Washington, D.C. (Hoover's, 2016). Through its Reach Media division, it operates its nationally syndicated programs, which include: The Tom Joyner Morning Show, The Ricky Smiley Morning Show, The Yolanda Adams Morning Show, The Russ Parr Morning Show, and The D.L. Hughley Morning Show (Yahoo! Finance, 2009). It's Interactive One division is the company's online business platform; and TV One is their online television division (Yahoo! Finance, 2009).

Recently, Radio One filed a trademark application for "Urban One," which will provide business promotion services; continue its radio, television, and internet offerings; and provide community engagement opportunities (Network Business Weekly, 2016). With Radio One's national multi-media platform, the company could continue expanding by collaborating with African media. A model they could follow for this is the collaboration

between MTV's "Staying Alive" campaign and The Henry J.

Kaiser Family Foundation, the United Nations Program on AIDS

(UNAIDS), the United Nations Children's Fund (UNICEF), and

the United Nations Population Fund (UNFPA), which produced the

popular Kenyan television show "Shuga," to promote HIV/AIDS

awareness and prevention (Boston University, 2016). According to

UNICEF (2016), the show began in Kenya as ". . . three-part series

revolving around six university friends, explor[ing] issues of sexual

relationships, and the ramifications of sexual decisions" (p. 5).

Since then, the show has grown from a three-part series to four full

seasons, with season four being filmed in Lagos, Nigeria (Africa

News Service, 2016).

    Radio One can assist in like manner by partnering with

African radio and television producers who seek to promote

content that is socially responsible and for the purpose of

community empowerment. With this in mind, Radio One could

partner with Brand South Africa's "Play Your Part" campaign, which began in 2011 as a means of highlighting inspiring stories of ordinary citizens working for the improvement of their communities (Africa News Service, 2011 & Play Your Part, 2016). Radio One could expand the campaign by spotlighting the international cooperation and community building by African-Americans and Africans throughout Africa and the Diaspora; covering the expanded services through their TV One asset.

SET Enterprises

Specializing in metal processing and duct manufacturing services for the automotive industry for over 25 years, SET Enterprises has its corporate headquarters in Warren, Michigan; and is led by President and CEO, Victor Edozien (SET, 2015). In addition to providing metal processing services, the company also provides heating, ventilation, and air conditioning (HVAC) ducts used to ensure indoor air quality; and polyvinyl coated ductwork exhaust, which manages underground fumes and air delivery systems (Bloomberg, 2016 & HRANEC, 2016).

With their capacity to compete in the auto and HVAC markets, SET has the potential to partner in Africa's infrastructure development. To explain, by 2022, the high demand for mini-split air conditioning units in the North African HVAC market is expected to generate over $891.48 billion (Research and Markets, 2015). This could be due to reforms taking place in the North African housing finance sector, which is slowly transitioning from direct state control to a more market-based approach (Centre for Affordable Housing, 2012). This is especially true for Morocco and Tunisia, where the housing finance market is most developed (McVitty, 2013). Mortgage spending in Morocco and Tunisia equals 17% and 12% of their GDP, and is expected to increase 5% and 12% per year (McVitty, 2013).

The growth in the HVAC market is also due to the amount of home construction occurring in North Africa. Egypt for example, needs 500,000 homes a year to be built in order to meet demand (Africa Property News, 2014). Algeria has a demand for 200,000 to 250,000 housing units to be built per year (Centre for

Affordable Housing, 2015). Libya has a housing shortage of 350,000; and with war continuing in the country, the need will certainly grow (Centre for Affordable Housing, 2015). In Morocco, annual housing production is approximately 100,000 units, and in 2014 they experienced a housing deficit of 650,000 units (Centre for Affordable Housing, 2015). South Sudan has virtually no housing industry due to political unrest, though investors have expressed interest (Centre for Affordable Housing, 2015). Tunisia also has an annual housing demand of 77,000 housing units (Centre for Affordable Housing, 2015).

SET can share in this growth opportunity by signing memoranda of understanding and contract partnerships with the primary developers in North Africa to provide HVAC services. For instance, in Morocco, they could partner with Al-Omrane, a state-owned land developer (Centre for Affordable Housing, 2015). They also could partner with Addoha, one of Morocco's largest developers, accounting for almost half of all low-cost housing being constructed in the country (Centre for Affordable Housing,

2015). In Egypt, they could partner with Arabtec, which plans to build one-million homes over a 13-year period (Africa Property News, 2014).

Africa south of the Sahara also presents opportunity for growth and development. In May, 2015, the International Finance Corporation and Chinese Engineering and Construction Company (CITIC), launched the $300 million investment platform CITIC (Africa) Holding Limited; to develop affordable housing in multiple countries throughout Africa (International Finance Corporation, 2015). With Kenya and Nigeria having priority, the plan is to engender cooperation between the local housing development companies, and provide them with long-term capital to develop 30,000 homes over the next five-years (International Finance Corporation, 2015). SET could join this platform; serving the local developers with their HVAC products.

Conclusions

Between African-Americans and Africa, there is significant room for economic engagement. The risk factors and infrastructure concerns associated with investing in Africa should not disqualify the continent as a whole from being a viable location for African-American businesses to globalize. To participate in the explosive growth transpiring on the continent, African-American business owners should attend conferences of intergovernmental bodies that African governments have memberships in such as: the African Union, the African Development Bank, the West African Development Bank, the United Nations, the Southern Africa Development Community (SADC), the Common Market for Eastern and Southern Africa (COMESA), the Economic Community of West African States (ECOWAS), the Economic Community of Central African States (ECCAS), and the Intergovernmental Authority for Development (IGAD) among many others. They should also join think tanks that research the political, social, and economic climate in Africa to remain abreast of the developments that could result in economic cooperation. Having the most capital among African-American businesses, the ten described in the research could serve as a forerunner for smaller African-American owned firms to establish a foothold on the continent. By conducting research and analysis of potential new African markets—eliminating those that are less attractive and acting on those that are more attractive (Grunig & Morschett, 2012)—they can create a path for smaller African-American owned firms to traverse over time. Such cooperation can demonstrate to the general African-American populous that returning home to Africa can be more than an opportunity for cultural development, but economic development as well.

References

Andriamananjara, S. (2015, June). Understanding the Importance of Tripartite Trade Area.

Brookings Institute. Retrieved from brookings.edu/blogs/africa-in-focus/posts/2015/06/17-tripartitite-free-trade-area-andriamananjara

Anderson and Dubose, Inc (2016) (.). Austin: Dun and Bradstreet, Inc. Retrieved from

http://search.proquest.com/docview/230570025?accountid=458

Black Enterprise. (2013) *The Nation's Largest Black Businesses*. Retrieved from http://www.blackenterprise.com/lists/be-100s-2014/.

Centre for Affordable Housing Finance in Africa. (2012). North Africa Regional Profile 2012, 1. Retrieved from http://www.housingfinanceafrica.org/document/north-africa-regional-profile/

Centre for Affordable Housing Finance in Africa. (2015). *2015 Yearbook-Housing Finance in Africa: A Review of Some of*

Africa's Housing Finance Markets, (06), 25–202. Retrieved
from http://www.housingfinanceafrica.org/document/2015-
housing-finance-in-africa-yearbook/

Central Intelligence Agency. (2016, June 6). The World Factbook:
Nigeria. Retrieved from
https://www.cia.gov/library/publications/the-world-
factbook/geos/ni.html

Chili's, D. (2016). Locations. Retrieved from
http://www.chilis.com/en/pages/locationslisting.aspx?Aspx
AutoDetectCookieSupport=1

Corral, P., Molini, V., & Oseni, G. (2015). No Condition is
Permanent: Middle Class in Nigeria in the Last Decade.
Policy Research Working Paper 7214, Volume (1), 7.
Retrieved from
http://documents.worldbank.org/curated/en/2015/03/241591
01/no-condition-permanent-middle-class-nigeria-last-decade#

Edmond Jr., A. (2011, December). UBR Spotlight: Quick-Service
Food Franchise Mogul Ulysses Bridgeman. *Black*

Enterprise. Retrieved from

http://www.blackenterprise.com/small-business/ubr-

spotlight-quick-service-food-franchise-mogul-ulysses-

bridgeman/

Egypt in need of half a million homes a year. (2014, November

27). *AfricaPropertyNews.com.* Retrieved from

http://www.africapropertynews.com/north-africa/3033-

egypt-in-need-of-half-a-million-homes-a-year.html

Ezeokoli , A. (2016, January 13). "MTV Shuga - Fusing HIV

Messaging With Entertainment to Help Fight Aids to the

Finish [Blog]." *Africa News Service. Opposing Viewpoints

in Context.* Web. May 2016.

Fast 50: Fastest Growing Companies. (2015, September 8).

Crane's Detroit Business. Retrieved from

http://www.crainsdetroit.com/article/20150809/AWARDS1

415/150809883/20-global-automotive-alliance-llc

Gallup, Inc., A. (2015). Global Law and Order 2015. *GALLUP.*

Retrieved from

http://www.gallup.com/services/185798/gallup-global-law-order-2015-report.aspx

Grunig, R., & Morschett, M. (2012). *Developing International Strategies: Going and Being International for Medium-sized Companies*. Springer. Retrieved from http://www.springer.com/us/book/9783642247248

Hoover's. (2016). Radio One, Inc. Retrieved from http://cobrands.hoovers.com

HRANEC Sheet Metal Inc. (2016, May 1). PVC Ductwork. Retrieved from hranec.com/ductwork-pcd.htm

Institute For Development Studies. (2016). Can Digital Jobs Solve Africa's Unemployment Crisis?, (13). Retrieved from https://www.ids.ac.uk/publication/can-digital-jobs-solve-africa-s-unemployment-crisis

International Labor Organization. (2016). World Employment and Social Outlook 2016, 29–31. Retrieved from http://www.ilo.org/global/research/global reports/weso/2016/WCMS_443480/lang--en/index.htm

Juwaheer, T. D., Pudaruth, S., & Ramdin, P. (2013). Enhancing

customer shopping experience in malls of emerging

countries – the "Mauritius" experience. *World Journal of

Entrepreneurship, Management and Sustainable

Development, 9*(2), 178–190. Retrieved from

http://www.emeraldinsight.com/doi/abs/10.1108/WJEMSD

-01-2013-0005

Kalumiya, N., & Kannon, A. P. (2015). Mauritius 2015, 5–9.

Retrieved from http://www.africaneconomicoutlook.org/

Mauritius Attractions. (2016). Shopping in Mauritius. Retrieved

from https://mauritiusattractions.com/shopping-in-

mauritius-i-91.html

Mauritius Ministry of Finance & Economic Development. (2016).

Monthly Tourist Arrival. Retrieved from

http://statsmauritius.govmu.org/English/Publications/Pages/

Monthly-Tourist-Arrival.aspx

McVitty, J. (2013). North Africa Regional Profile 2013, 2.

Retrieved from

http://www.housingfinanceafrica.org/document/north-africa-regional-profile-2/

Modise , O. M., & Mosweunyane , D. M. (2014). International briefing 32: training and development in Botswana. *International Journal of Training and Development, 18*(4), 303. doi:10.1111

National Automotive Council: Federal Ministry of Industry, Trade, and Investment. (2014). Information Document on the Nigerian Automotive Industry Development Plan, 4. Retrieved from http://www.naddc.gov.ng/AUTO_POLICY_INFO_DOC.pdf

Ndulu, B. J., & O'Connell, S. A. (2010). Chapter 1. In *Policy plus: African Growth Performance, 1960–2000* (p. 2). Cambridge University Press. doi:http://dx.doi.org/10.1017/CBO9780511492648.002

Newpoff, L. (2015, December 17). Top of the List: Biggest minority-owned businesses. *Columbus Business First.* Retrieved from

http://www.bizjournals.com/columbus/blog/2015/12/top-of-

the-list-biggest-minority-owned-businesses.html

North Africa HVAC Market, 2015-2022 - Forecast & Analysis.

(2015). *Research and Markets*, 1–159. Retrieved from

http://www.researchandmarkets.com/research/hp9zhz/north_af

rica_hvac

Ohio Manufacturer's Association. (2013, June 21). Bio – Billy

Vickers, Modular Assembly Innovations. Retrieved from

http://www.ohiomfg.com/grip-assets/pdf/2013-06-

21_lb_lead_billy-vickers-bio.pdf

"Play Your Part TV Series Set to Inspire." *Africa News Service* 22

Oct. 2011. *Opposing Viewpoints in Context*. Web. 8 June 2016.

Play Your Part. (2016, April 22). Play Your Part TV series.

Retrieved from http://www.playyourpart.co.za/tv-series-news

PriceWaterCooper. (2016). Africa's Next Automotive Hub, 7–23.

Retrieved from

https://www.pwc.com/ng/en/assets/pdf/africas-next-

automotive-hub.pdf

Rockefeller Foundation. (2013). Digital Jobs Africa, 1. Retrieved

from

https://www.rockefellerfoundation.org/app/uploads/Digital-

Jobs-Africa.pdf

SET Enterprises. (2015). About Us. Retrieved from

http://www.setenterprises.com/about

Smith, J. (2006). *Encyclopedia of African-American Business

Volume 1*. Greenwood Publishing Group. Retrieved from

https://books.google.com/

Spiropolous, R. (2014, August). Spotlight on Africa: How African

American Entrepreneurs Can Engage. Black Enterprise.

Retrieved from http://www.blackenterprise.com/small-

business/us-africa-summit-african-american-entrepreneurs-

tips-part-2/

Stines, A. (2016, January 15). Top of the List: Louisville's largest

minority-owned businesses. *Louisville Business First*.

Retrieved from

http://www.bizjournals.com/louisville/blog/2016/01/top-of-

the-list-minority-owned-businesses.html

The Act 1 Group Inc. (2016). (). Austin: Dun and Bradstreet, Inc.

Retrieved from

http://search.proquest.com/docview/230544102?accountid=458

The Anderson-Dubose Company. (2013). Retrieved from

www.anderson-dubose.com/inform/about.php

The Heritage Foundation. (2016). 2016 Index of Economic

Freedom: Botswana. Retrieved from

http://www.heritage.org/index/country/botswana

The World Bank. (2016, April 12). Overview of Botswana.

Retrieved from

http://www.worldbank.org/en/country/botswana/overview#1

Thompson Hospitality Corporation. (2016).( ).Austin: Dun and

Bradstreet Inc. Retrieved from

http://search.proquest.com/docview/230607437?accountid=

35812

Thompson Hospitality. (2015).( ).Costa Mesa: Experian

Information Solutions, Inc. Retrieved from

http://search.proquest.com/docview/1574921729?accountid

=35812

Trademarks; an application for the trademark "URBAN ONE" has

been filed by radio one. (2016). *Network Business Weekly,*

791. Retrieved from

http://search.proquest.com/docview/1764403987?accountid=458

University of Botswana. (2008, February 20). Learning and

Teaching Policy. Retrieved from

http://www.ub.bw/ip/documents/Learning%20and%20Teac

hing%20Policy.pdf

U.S. Census Bureau. (2011, February 8). Census Bureau Reports

the Number of Black-Owned Businesses Increased at Triple

the National Rate. *Newsroom Archive.* Retrieved from

https://www.census.gov/newsroom/releases/archives/busine

ss_ownership/cb11-24.html

Warde, B. (2014). Why Race Still Matters 50 years After the Enactment of the 1964 Civil Rights Act. Journal of African American Studies, 18(2), 251–259. doi:10.1007/s12111-013-9264-3.

Weeks, M. W. (2013, September 4). Minority buying power grows in 2013, according to Selig Center report. *University of Georgia: Terry College Business*, p. 1.

World Health Organization: Country Planning Cycle Database. (2009). "10th National Development Plan 2009-2016." *Botswana: National Health Planning Cycles*. Retrieved from http://www.nationalplanningcycles.org/planning-cycle/BWA

World Trade Organization. (2015, December 16). President Kenyatta hails approval by ministers of Liberia's WTO membership. *WTO: 2015 NEWS ITEMS*. Retrieved from https://www.wto.org/english/news_e/news15_e/acc_lbr_16dec15_e.htm

Yahoo!Finance . (2016, June 18). Radio One Inc.Profile. Retrieved from https://finance.yahoo.com/q/pr?s=ROIA+Profile

Closing the Educational Achievement Gap Between Blacks and Whites: Nobody Wants to be Black

2006

Statistics from the U.S Census Bureau confirm that there is an economic advantage for African-Americans who hold a four-year degree. It also shows that possession of a four-year degree increases the incomes of African-Americans and almost closes the economic gap between African-Americans and Caucasians. African-Americans with a four-year college degree now earn on average twice the income of African-Americans who have no better than a high-school diploma. In 2003, African-American women with a Bachelor's degree had a median income of $33,142, 110 percent of the $30,082 median income for Caucasian women who held a college degree (JBHE News & Views, 2005, p. 4).

Education is the key to limitless opportunities for social, economic, and political upward mobility in contemporary society. However, a vast disparity exists between the number of African-Americans and Caucasians who are attaining four-year college degrees. Several factors within the African-American race contribute to the educational achievement gap: lack of parental involvement in their children's education because of family structure and education level, the devaluation of education through alternative methods of acquiring income, and the lack of personal responsibility of the parents for not instilling in their children the value of education and the opportunity that it produces. Factors that contribute to the educational achievement gap outside of the Black race include: BET (Black Entertainment Television), the media's belittlement of education for the African-American race, and the partial regulatory practices of the Federal Communications Commission.

This paper describes the educational achievement gap, the causes of the achievement gap, the consequences of the achievement gap, and possible solutions to close the educational achievement gap.

Description of the Educational Achievement Gap between Blacks and Whites

A high school diploma is essential in closing the educational achievement gap on the collegiate level. If African-American students do not complete high school successfully with their diploma, the chances of them being able to enroll in a college/university are constricted, thus not having the opportunity to aid in closing the educational achievement gap. In 2003, 20 percent of Blacks dropped out of high school, compared to 11 percent of Whites, and 35 percent of Blacks completed high school compared to 33 percent of Whites. In 2004, 11.8 percent of Blacks dropped out of high school, compared to 6.8 percent of Whites (U.S 2004). On the collegiate level, according to the U.S Census 2003, 36.4 million people in the United States are classified as Black, of these, 3,854,000, or less than 11 percent, hold a four-year college degree. Only 1 in 9 African-Americans possess a four-year degree (JBHE News & Views 2005 p. 4). According to the National Center for Education Statistics, in 2003 12 percent of Blacks had attained a bachelor's degree compared to 20 percent of Whites.

Data from the consortium for Student Retention Data Exchange (SRDE) indicate that African-American students are dropping out of post-secondary school in great numbers during their junior and senior years. The overall graduation rate for African-Americans after six years is 38 percent compared with 56 percent for Caucasian students (USA Funds Education Access 2004 pp. 1-2). In 2004, only 1,276,000 African-Americans were at college level compared to 7,138,000 of their Caucasian counterparts (U.S Census, 2006). Enrollment for African-Americans was 63 percent compared to 64 percent for Caucasians. In 2005, 18 percent of Blacks graduated with a Bachelor's degree compared to 38 percent of Whites.

The Benefits of Parental Involvement

Parental involvement in a child's education is a necessity to the child's life. It not only aids them to excel in school, but cultivates an appreciation of education, which would drive to feel confident in attending college and acquire a four-year degree. Also,

At home, children may learn the type of relationship to authority that facilitates good rapport with teachers. Ability to follow directions, have long attention span, are success in verbal comprehension, ability to grasp relationships between things, and ability to do school work with diligence may also be influenced by home training (Ogbu, 1978, p. 20).

The Northwest Regional Educational Library defines parental involvement as "the active, ongoing participation of a child's parent(s) or guardian(s) in their education" (NREL 1999). Moreover, a study conducted by Phi Delta Kappan in 1980 disclosed that, "[P]arental representation in the urban school served as a significant factor in procuring positive results . . . [O]ther researchers have also reported that children whose parents are involved in their schooling can make an appreciable increase in the child's academic achievement" (Trotman, 2001, p. 277). Also, according to the Journal of Higher Education, "Parental involvement is associated with a greater likelihood of aspiring to attend college and actually enrolling as well as with higher eight grade mathematics and reading achievement, lower rates of behavioral problems, and lower likelihood of high school dropout and truancy" (Perna & Titus, 2005, p. 486).

Contributing Factors within the Black Race:
The Lack of Parental Involvement and Family Structure

Despite the research that has proven the benefits of parental involvement; a lack of African-American parental involvement is still prevalent. This is due to the deterioration of the family structure. According to Trotman (2001, p. 279),

> The nuclear family structure of father, mother, and children has seen a dramatic decrease. An increasing number of families are headed by a single-parent, especially in urban settings (Lippman, et al., 1996). This phenomenon has occurred as a result of surges in the number of divorces, separations, and unwed and/or teenage pregnancies. Fewer school-aged children come from two-parent, single-wage earner families.

There are two theories that attempt to explain the family's effect on a child's education both from Biblarz and Raftery (1999, pp. 324-325). The first theory is the Learning theory, which views the family as,

[A] primary site where children learn about how to get along in the society when they reach adulthood (Kohn 1969, 1983). Without a father, children lack a male model of how to successfully achieve market activity (Powell and Parcel 1997; McLanahan and Sandefur 1994). In two-biological parent families, children learn about how authority relations are structured and how to successfully interact with authority figures (Nock 1988). This learning facilitates children's educational and occupational attainment. Children reared in single-parent families from birth have roughly an equal high school dropout rate as those who experienced a transition mother-father to a single-parent family following divorce.

According to the *Economic theory*, children's success depends upon,

[T]he economic resources and the equivalent services that parents provide, children who spend most of their childhoods in a two-parent family (biological or step) will have the highest attainments because two parental figures are present to provide complementary resources. Single-parent families will yield less income from the market and have less time for the provision of household services. One-parent cannot cover both market and non-market activities as successfully as two, and children from single-parent families, accordingly, do less well . . . Children who grow up in single-mother families will have the lowest attainments-mother-headed families average less than a third of the income of two parent families and about half of the income alternative father-headed families. This implies that the single-mother will be too occupied with generating income to support the household to be actively engaged in her child's education. With the single-mother's income being the only income of the household, funding for additional activities such as filed trips, summer camps-let alone college, are extremely limited. This also implies that mother-headed families are often living in poverty.

According to the Census 2000 Special Reports, the poverty rate for children under 18 years old living in mother-only homes for African-Americans was 47.4 percent, compared to 28.1 percent of Caucasians.

Another reason why African-American parents are lacking participation in their child's education is because of their education level. According to the Journal of Higher Education,

Specifically descriptive analyses show that African-Americans and Hispanics not only average lower levels of family income, parental education, and math coursework, than Whites and Asian Americans, but also are relatively concentrated in schools in the lowest quartiles of average family income and parental education. For example, 37% of African-Americans and 49% of Hispanics attend schools in the lowest quartile of parental education, compared with 17% Caucasians and16% Asian Americans. (Perna & Titus, 2005, p. 509)

Because of this disparity in parental education, parents may be discouraged from active participation in the schools by teachers, administration, and their own inferiority complex.

Alternative Methods of Acquiring Income: Sports

The second factor that contributes to the educational achievement gap within the African-American race is the existence of alternative methods of acquiring income through professional sports (Basketball and Baseball) and drug trafficking. The average salary of an NBA player is 4.17 million, which surpasses an average $72,741 an African-American with a Ph.D. earns (NBA Players Association). For instance, in 2005 more high-school seniors were taken into the National Basketball Association lottery (draft) than college graduates (Chalfin 2006). A small sample of these individuals that are currently in the NBA include: Kobe Bryant, Lebron James, and Josh Smith. Concerning baseball, the average salary of a baseball player is $2.6 million. There were 90 African-Americans in the major leagues and only 34 of them possess a college degree (Verducci 2003).

Alternative Methods of Acquiring Income: Drugs

Drug-dealing (especially in cocaine and marijuana) offers an alternative method of acquiring income to a college degree. According to the Journal of Qualitative Sociology, "Drug-dealing offers the promise of lavish lifestyles otherwise unattainable to most ghetto youth and other impoverished groups. Dealing also provides an alternative to low-paying dead-end jobs typically available to those with little education and few skills" (Murphy, Waldorf, and Reinarman 1990, p. 336).

For the African-American drug dealer seeking to reach cartel status, the aspiration is to make between $250-$300 million every year—like Carl Ledher (Moushey 1996). On the low-end is the drug dealer who is trying to make enough profit simply to sustain his/her habit or status. In either case, because he/she is not in college pursuing a degree, they are contributing to the educational achievement gap. According to the Drug Control Strategy Update 2003, 25 percent of African-American state prisoners or approximately 122,000 inmates were serving time for drug-possession, trafficking, or other unspecified drug offenses. By comparison, among Caucasian inmates this proportion was 11.8 percent or approximately 40,900.

Alternative Methods of Acquiring Income: The Lack of Personal Responsibility

The lack of personal responsibility is a factor contributing to the educational achievement gap within the African-American race because it curtails dedication to education. It is responsible for causing students to drop out of school and live lives of limited opportunity. According to the National Center for Education Statistics 2003, 20 percent of African-Americans dropped out of high school compared to 11 percent of Caucasians. In 2004, 11.8 percent of African-Americans dropped out of high school compared to 6.8 percent of Caucasians (U.S Census, 2006). If African-American students are not attaining their high school diplomas, they have a very limited chance to compete on the college level. They cannot compete because of the majority of college/universities in the public sector will not admit a student without their high school diploma or GED (General Education Development). Without the opportunity to attend a public college/university and the funds to pay for an education at a private institution, the opportunities for quality selection of housing and jobs are constricted. Once these opportunities are closed, the only life that remains is too often the life of drugs, crime, prostitution, eventual incarceration, or residence in the slums, as the following case studies from Dunlap, Golub, Johnson (2006, pp. 127-133) of "Ricochet," "Island," and her two children, "Sonya" and "Ross" demonstrate this point,

> At age 18 Ricochet [from Brooklyn, NY] dropped out of school. She started dating a man she met while he was installing new door bells in her apartment building. They had a daughter together, Tushay, but the relationship did not last long. He said that he was in his twenties. However, he was actually almost 40 and already married. Ricochet would leave care of the child to her mother. At 19, she was in the prime of life. She had a large circle of friends. She

knew what was happening, she attended parties, drank alcohol, smoked marijuana and started to smoke cocaine free-base. It was 1980, and her life was fun and care free . . . At 21 Ricochet became romantically involved with John, who had just returned from jail to live with his mother in the apartment above Joyce's [Ricochet's mother]. Ricochet and John had a daughter together, Fruit Loops. John was a heroin addict and mostly hustled to support his habit. He was also very violent. To protect herself, Ricochet would call the police, "I kept him locked up [To keep him] from beating me all the time . . . Families often waited for months and even years for a run-down apartment, most often in housing projects. Given their lack of income and lack of discipline in paying rent and bills, many families did not remain in their units long. Once Ricochet set up her own household, there was a steady parade of boyfriends and other short-term relationships. Ricochet was spending even less time with her children and more time with her crack-habit. Ricochet reported, "I used to smoke up all my money. I was getting like $311 cash in the projects . . . ." Tushay recalled, "I call the BCW [Bureau of Child Welfare] on my mother when she didn't buy me no school clothes . . . She didn't even feed me for like two days." Indeed Ricochet's mother, Joyce, as well as her two children Tushay and Fruitloops all called BCW at different times to complain about Ricochet's inattentive parenting. After a few years, Ricochet lost the apartment for not paying the rent . . . .

Island Bersini chose her pseudonym because she was born in the Islands. Island's story of lacking personal responsibility is divergent from Ricochet's in that the case study does not indicate that she went to high school. Nevertheless, because she did not have an education, she could not value it enough to pass it on to her two children, Sonya and Ross, and this was the result,

Sonya reached age 17 in 1970, during the peak years of the Heroin Era. After her initial introduction to the drug, Sonya quickly became addicted. She left high school and married a heroin addict and dealer. She and her husband lived in shooting galleries. Sonya raised additional money as a prostitute. After a few years, they separated and he moved to Florida. Soon afterward, Sonya was arrested and sent to prison for participating in the robbery of a jewelry store with a friend. After release, Sonya returned to live with Island. While imprisoned, she had gotten clean from heroin. In the 1980's, Sonya started using crack and again quickly became dependent. Her life revolved around her habit. Whenever she had any money, she would smoke crack. Her main income came from prostitution. As soon as she would turn a trick and make a few dollars, she would find a dealer, buy some crack, and smoke, sometimes she would directly exchange sex-for-crack, avoiding dealing with the money and having to find a dealer.

Island's second-child, Ross, also became part of the street scene. As a child, he always hated being poor and felt stigmatized by public assistance. At age 16, he dropped out of school to try to support the family by selling PCP. Ross married at age 18. Soon afterwards, he was arrested for dealing and sent to prison for two years. Upon release, he returned to Island's household, rather than to his wife, and returned to selling marijuana and PCP. In 1975, he started selling heroin but hated the drug because of what happened to his sister. Heroin had become known as one of the worst, if not the worst drug on the street. When the police increased their pressure on dealers, Ross was arrested and sent to prison for another two years. After release, he was shot during a robbery. As a result, he was paralyzed and confined to a wheelchair for the rest of his life. His condition, however, did not stop him from dealing drugs. Even though he was still legally married, Ross began living with another woman, Gladys, who bore three children by him. . . . Eventually, however, Ross moved back in with Island.

Contributing Factors Outside of the Black Race: The Media and how they Belittle Education for the African-Americans

The media also is a contributor outside of the African-American race to the educational achievement gap because it consistently depicts African-Americans as a race of uneducated, drug-dealing thugs; not as scholarly, degree seeking people. For example, Boost mobile is the self-proclaimed cell-phone company for today's youth, and the individuals they used to promote their "Anthem" campaign (a music-video commercial) included Hip-Hop "artists" such as "Ludacris," "Kanye West," and "The Game"—rappers who promote money, sex, and drugs in their music. Also, their slogan is, "Where You At?" which is a grammatically unsound question (Boost, 2006).

Black Entertainment Television

BET contributes to the educational achievement gap because they give these Hip-Hop "artists" who promote money, sex, drugs, and violence, an outlet through which their voice can be heard. According to BET's executive communications department, approximately 80 million people watch BET's programs daily (BET's Executive Communications Department, personal correspondence, July, 2006). In fact, BET airs 18 hours of explicit music videos per six days out of the week compared to 30 minutes of the reality series "College Hill," which follows the lives of eight college co-eds (BET and TV, 2006). How hours of music videos televised were calculated,

> *106 & Park* is aired Monday-Friday 6:00-7:30 pm and on Saturday 11:00-12:30 p.m. and 6:00 p.m.-7:30 p.m. *Rap City* is aired Monday-Friday 5:00-6:00 p.m. *College Hill* is aired Thursdays at 9:00-9:30 p.m.
>
> 1hr 30 min x 5 days (Monday-Friday) = 9hrs; 3hrs x 1 day (Saturday) = 3hrs
>
> **Total number of hours for *106 & Park* =12 hrs**
>
> 1 hr x 5 days (Monday-Friday) = 6 hours
>
> **Total number of hours for *Rap City* = 6 hours**
>
> Total hrs of *106 & Park* (12) + Total hrs of *Rap City* (6) =
>
> 18 hours
>
> **Total hours of music videos aired = 18 hours**

Therefore, if BET is sponsoring rappers such as "TI," who glories in the financial benefits of selling crack in his song, "What you know," on his latest platinum album (1 million units sold) entitled, "King," and also awarding TI, "Best Male Hip-Hop Artist of the Year" in 2006, then approximately 80 million people are being influenced to engage in that destructive lifestyle—a lifestyle which is contrary to acquiring a high school diploma and a bachelor's degree (Boston, 2006; Billboard 2006). BET's function as a microphone for Hip-Hop "artists" to be heard not only demotes education, but also violates two United Nations resolutions. The first is a resolution condemning genocide, which states,

> Having considered the declaration made by the General Assembly of the United Nations in its resolution 96(I) dated 11 December 1946 that genocide is a crime under international law, contrary to the spirit and aims of the United Nations and condemned by the civilized world.

Article 2

. . . genocide means any of the following acts committed with intent to destroy, in whole or in part, a natural, ethnical, racial, or religious group, as such:

(a)   Killing members of the group.

(b)   Causing serious bodily or mental harm to members of the group.

(c)   Deliberately inflicting on the group conditions of life calculated to bring about its physical destruction in whole or in part.

Article 4

Persons committing genocide or any other acts enumerated in article III shall be punished, whether they are constitutionally responsible rulers, public officials, or private individuals. (Convention on the Prevention and Punishment of the Crime of Genocide)

The second United Nations resolution that BET violates is the *Declaration on the Promotion and Youth of the Ideals of Peace, Mutual Respect and Understanding between Peoples*, which states,

Reaffirming the principles embodied in the General Assembly resolution 110 (II) of 3 November 1947 condemning all forms of propaganda designed or likely to provoke or encourage any threat to peace. Convinced furthermore that the education of the young and exchanges of young people and of ideas in a spirit of peace, mutual respect and understanding between peoples can help to improve international relations and to strengthen peace and security:

Principle 1

Young people shall be brought up in the spirit of peace, justice, freedom, mutual respect, and understanding in order to promote equal rights for all human beings and all nations, economic progress, disarmament of international peace and security.

Principle VI

A major aim in educating the young shall be to develop all their faculties and to train them to acquire higher moral qualities, to be deeply attached to the noble ideas of peace, liberty, the dignity and quality of all men, and imbued with respect and love for humanity and its creative achievements. To this end the family has an important role to play (General Assembly).

If BET can continue their operation unscathed by these resolutions and unregulated by the Federal Communications Commission (as the following section shows), and the rappers they promote can continue to make millions from of their music that glorifies everything contrary to education, then what is the incentive for African-Americans to complete high school with a diploma and graduate from college with a degree?

The Federal Communications Commission and Their Partial Regulatory Practices

The Federal Communications Commission is a contributor outside of the African-American race to the educational achievement gap because of its partiality in the regulation of television programs. The "Shock Jock," Howard Stern has been fined approximately $700,000 (1992 and 2004) by the FCC for his graphic dialogue and sexual exploitation of Caucasian women on his television show (CNN, 2004; NY Times, 1992). The FCC has also fined the Columbia Broadcasting System (CBS television) a record $3.6 million for a sexually graphic portrayal of teenage boys and girls engaging in an orgy on the television show "Without a Trace." Though they fine these stations for their offenses, the FCC has done absolutely nothing to curtail the sexually explicit acts and graphic images of African-Americans on BET. Since the FCC is allowing BET to continue their operation, they are allowing the demotion of education by the rappers' promotion of money, sex, drugs, and violence to continue the cycle of genocide. If society is relaying to the African-American community that education is not the way, then what incentive is there for African-Americans to aid in closing the educational achievement gap between themselves and Caucasians by pursuing and attaining a bachelor's degree?

Consequences of the Educational Achievement Gap for Blacks: Incarceration Rates of African-Americans

As previously stated, a lack of education (high school diploma and bachelor's degree) is associated with crime and imprisonment. In 2005, an estimated 12 percent of Black males in their late twenties were in prison or in jail compared to 1.7 percent of their White counterparts. At midyear 2005 Blacks were nearly five times more likely than Whites to have been in jail. Among the nearly 2.2 million offenders incarcerated on June 30, 2005, an estimated 548,300 were Black males between the ages of 20-39. Of Black non-Hispanic males ages 25 to 29, 11.9 percent were in prison or jail compared to approximately 1.7 percent of White males in the same age group. The incarceration rates for Blacks of all ages were 5 to 7 times greater than those for White males in the same age groups. The incarceration rate for Black non-Hispanic females was 347 per 100,000, 4 times higher than the rate for White females which is 88 per 100,000. These differences among White and Black females are consistent across all age groups (U.S Dept. of Justice, 2005, pp.1-13). Black male juveniles 16-24 totaled 2,757,448 from 1990-2004, compared to 12,017,952 of their White counterparts (Office of Juvenile Justice, 2004[1]).

African-American Poverty

According to the aforesaid, a powerful economic advantage accrues to African-Americans who hold a four-year degree. African-Americans who earn bachelor's degrees earn twice the income of those with merely a high-school diploma (JBHE News & Views, 2005, p. 4). However, not possessing a college degree has direct correlation with poverty. According to the U.S Census Bureau 2005, there are 36,423,000 African-Americans in the U.S.

---

[1]The Bureau of Justice Statistics could not provide statistics detailing the exact percentage of Black and White inmates with college degrees.

Of that 36,423,000, 32,515,000 do not have college degrees; of that 32,515,000, 8,723,000 are living in poverty. There are 36, 423, 000 African-Americans in the U.S; of that number, 17,473,000 African-Americans ages 25 and over do not have college degrees, and of that number 3,845,000 are living in poverty.[2] According to Dunlap, Golub, and Johnson (2006, p.118),

> Poverty and long-term joblessness have been associated with a constellation of detrimental consequences: over-crowded housing, poor physical and mental wellness, despair, post-traumatic stress disorder, family dissolution, teen pregnancy, school dropout, crime, violence, interpersonal violence, and drug and alcohol abuse, among others.

The educational achievement gap and all its contributors have also

---

[2]Method of finding those in poverty without degrees:

Subtract: all educational levels, all incomes – 4-year degree or more, all income levels = number of African-Americans without a college degree

Subtract: all educational levels, below 100% of poverty – 4-year degree or more, below 100% poverty=number without degree in poverty. (U.S Census Bureau: Joe Dalaker, Poverty and Health Statistics Branch)

caused dissension between the descendants of Africa—African-Americans and the peoples of the Caribbean. It has caused the peoples of the Caribbean to not affiliate themselves with American Blacks. There are several reasons for this, according to Benjamin Bailey (2001, p. 689),

> Most studies on the identities of post 1965 Afro-Caribbean immigrants have focused on the first generation. The first generation overwhelmingly rejects the folk-racial categorization of "black American" that is imposed on them, instead emphasizing their ethnicity as Haitians, Jamaicans, Trinidadians, etc. Many in the first generation actively disassociate themselves from African Americans,
>
>> If race unites Jamaicans with American blacks, ethnicity divides them. Jamaicans . . . feel they are different then, indeed superior to, indigenous blacks and they conduct their social life mainly with other Jamaicans.

Ethnicity . . . while it draws them together with their fellow Jamaicans (and often other West Indians), it drives a deep wedge between them and American blacks

(Foner, 1987: 213-214).

. . . [There] also exists a subdivision of the second generation who hold to their parents' belief that Afro-Caribbean immigrants are [divergent] from African-Americans and superior in many respects and that, with perseverance, they can succeed socioeconomically regardless of racism. They have enough contact with white Americans and middle-class Americans to know that many whites and socially mobile Americans share this view that African descent immigrants are more industrious, disciplined and education oriented than other African descent Americans. They attribute their hard work in school and opportunities for mobility to the discipline and culture of their immigrant ethnicity.

Those from the Caribbean are also seen as superior because of the economic advantage that they are perceived to possess. According to the *Cultural* and *Demand* side arguments,

Caribbean Blacks are said to be higher achievers who have a greater work ethic compared to American Blacks. These immigrants have had greater opportunity to pursue individual economic endeavors in the past, both during and after slavery. Their socialization is a more favorable climate in the Caribbean, where they have always been a racial majority, also facilitated the development of a psyche that manifests itself in higher achievement relative to African-Americans (Glazer & Moynihan 1963; Lewis 1983; Sowell 1978) . . . Caribbean blacks are also said to benefit from favorable perceptions that white Americans and employers have about them, relative to African Americans (Foner 1985; Hossfeld 1994; Waters 19994a; Dodoo, 1997, pp. 529-530).

There is further evidence that suggests the existence of a type of chain recruitment among Caribbean Blacks, where Caribbean workers recruited others into an organization; and that "Black immigrants emphasize their foreign origins because they perceive that it conveys an advantage (Dodoo, 1997, p. 531). The media, in exploiting the educational achievement gap between Blacks and Whites, has also made an appreciable impact on how those from the Caribbean view African-Americans. In Benjamin Bailey's interview with Eva (Dominican-American, U.S born) states the anti-Black attitude by her mother: ". . . most African-Americans don't really do good, most of them if you see them selling drugs or something, that's what she thinks, that most African-Americans don't do good" (Bailey, 2001, p. 699). The anti-Black sentiments of the Dominican first-generation stem from immigrants who bring with them negative stereotypes of African-Americans, based on media depictions and what they hear from friends and relatives in the United States. Teenagers that Benjamin Bailey interviewed in the Dominican Republic, who never had personal contact with African-Americans, associated them with gangs, crime, success in sports, and poverty (Bailey, 2001, p. 700).

Moreover, according to Benjamin Bailey (2001, p. 700), "Newly immigrated Dominicans, hoping to make a better life for themselves have little incentive to have dealings with a group that is viewed to be among the least socially and economically mobile in America. The anti-black sentiment is portrayed even in the policy of categorizing races in that country." Benjamin Bailey (2001, pp. 677, 696) states,

> The majority of Dominicans have sub-Saharan African ancestry, which would make them "black" by historical United States 'one drop' rules . . . [Yet] Dominicans on the Island do not think of themselves as being black, but rather more or less European/Whites. In the Dominican Republic, perceived or imagined European ancestry makes an individual not black. By this measure, a small percentage of Dominicans are counted as black.

Regrettably, the research of Bailey is borne out in the author's personal experience. On July 31, 2006, the author (DC) journeyed to San Juan, Puerto-Rico to visit his sister "Rachel," an Afro-Latina, whom he had never met. He stayed there for ten days and experienced first-hand how "nappy" hair ("bad hair") and being African-American were viewed as undesirable by Puerto Rican society, as compared to the straight hair ("good hair") and light skin of the majority of Puerto-Ricans. The author can recall the racial profiling he experienced while on the island. One instance involved a visit to the local Sam's Mart with "Angel" (the hostess) and Rachel to purchase food supplies for the coming month. The author was stopped at the entrance to the store and questioned by the check-out clerk. Angel then intervened, and the author was allowed into the store.

Another occurrence of racial profiling transpired while the author, Angel, and Rachel were en route to the post-office. While walking, numerous Puerto-Ricans stared disapprovingly at the author and his sister. In the post-office, a child in close proximity to the author looked disdainfully at the author's sister because of her hair texture. The author was quite disturbed at how children were indoctrinated in the racist sentiments of Puerto-Rican culture. When questioned about this anti-Black phenomenon, the hostess explained that the racism of that culture towards African-Americans is learned from the preceding generations. She confirmed that her grandmother taught her to have no dealings with African-Americans because she considered them thugs, and how in her earlier life she was ostracized by her family for dating African-American men. With the educational achievement gap and all its contributing factors creating a stigma for the Black race—associating them with drug-dealing, crime, and poverty—what is there for the descendants of Africa in the Caribbean to have any affiliation with the African-American race?

Solutions to the Educational Achievement Gap: Parental Involvement

Though the educational achievement gap between Blacks and Whites is a detriment for the Black race, the wound is not incurable. The first solution is an accretion in parental involvement and school understanding. Johnetta B. Cole, president of Bennett College for Women asserts,

> Parental engagement is the No.1 reason why children demonstrate superior academic performance, then they learn to appreciate what education has to offer. Parental involvement must not stop there, however. Parents must volunteer to become active participants within their educational institutions. For instance, running for a seat on the local school board would be a good start. As an elected member, the opportunities, to influence everything from curriculum development to budgets abound. Parents could advocate for a national policy to encourage the Bush administration to enact new initiatives, but the most productive means of making a difference is on the school level, one school district at a time. (Meeks, 2005, p. 148)

Many parents are inhibited from participation in their child's education because of social, economic, or physical needs.

Teachers and administration must be willing to go the extra mile for parents, even if that entails providing transportation for parents to attend the Parent-Teacher Association meetings, and Parent-Teacher conferences. Trotman writes,

> It is important that educators recognize that both the child and the school benefit when the parents participate in either school-based or home-based activities. The child benefits by having both the school and home place emphasis on education, while the school benefits by being in partnership with parents who are supportive of their educational program. (2001, p. 276)

By children witnessing the collaboration between school and their parents, they will learn to value education, be more apt to graduate from high-school with a diploma, enroll in college, and graduate with a four-year degree, thus aiding in closing the educational achievement gap between African-Americans and Caucasians. Teachers can also aid the parents in closing the achievement gap ". . . by asking parents for their assistance, views, and suggestions, as a means to better prepare their child and ensure academic success" (Trotman, 2001, p. 278).

Solutions to the Educational Achievement Gap: After-School Programs and Pre-Collegiate Programs

A second possible solution is enrolling more African-American high-school students in after-school programs and pre-collegiate programs. The Extended Service Schools federal initiative is geared toward meeting the needs of the youth by providing developmental opportunities for children and adolescents. According to the ESS,

> School-based, after-school programs are increasingly becoming the solution to policy-makers suggest for all sorts of youth problems- poor-academic achievement, gang participation, violence, and drug-use. Federal spending alone for school-based, after-school programs has gone from $40 million in 1997 to a proposed $850 million in 2001. According to ESS, school-based programs, after-school programs are promising strategies for engaging

youth in a variety of positive social, recreational and academic activities. The programs hold the potential of providing young people with opportunities to develop skills, roles, and relationships essential to their ultimate success while also sheltering them during a time of vulnerability[they] observed that the programs did actively attract and engage thousands of children and youth who have few other positive options for filling their after-school time. [However,] they found it to be significantly easier to recruit elementary school children than middle and high school students. Among the early enrollees, 30 percent were in grade three or lower, 45 percent were in grades four to six, 25 percent were in grades seven or eight, and only 2 percent were in grades nine or higher [between 1998-1999].

[Some ESS programs] found that teens enjoyed organizing and participating in special events such as community service, neighborhood cleanups, running their own clubs, and working with younger youth as tutors, mentors, or ESS staff. Offering teen programs with flexible open-door policies, [coupled] with opportunities for leadership and loosely guided autonomy seemed most effective. Older youth were also attracted to programs that aided them with job readiness and placement. (Grossman, Walker, & Raley, pp. 3, 9-10, 15-16)

College preparation programs are still another way to aid in closing the educational achievement gap because they prepare African-Americans for the rigor of college life. According to Perna & Titus (2005, 485-486),

College preparation programs (also known as early intervention programs and pre-collegiate programs) are an increasingly common approach to raising the college enrollment rates of African Americans, Hispanics, and other groups of students who are underrepresented in higher education. [Such programs like TRIO, a federally funded collection of programs] are designed to promote educational attainment by developing the skills, knowledge, confidence, aspirations, and preparation that are needed to enroll in and graduate from college.

Consensus on the Importance of Education

The third solution for the African-American race is to come to the consensus that education is essential to the social and economic mobility of the race. Once this agreement has been reached, label all who demote, devalue, and oppose education, by promoting, valuing, and glorifying the corrupt use of money, sex, and drugs, as enemies of the African-American race. This also implies lobbying the Federal Communications Commission to place stricter regulations on Black Entertainment Television and Hip-Hop, and develop more television programs that promote African-American education and scholarship.

Summary

If the educational achievement gap between blacks and whites on the collegiate level does not minimize, the rate of black poverty, crime, and incarceration will continue to escalate; the perception of African-Americans as inferior by the general populous of the Caribbean will remain, and the opportunity for African upward mobility will remain constricted. In order for the educational achievement gap to minimize, the internal influences that negatively impact African-American education—single-parent homes, dependence upon sports, and drug-dealing—must be rectified. Additionally, the external factors that negatively impact education—the partial regulatory practices of the Federal Communications Commission, and promotion of genocide by BET—must be addressed. There must be a general consensus by the African-American race, that education is essential for upward mobility and all who are opposed to African-Americans acquiring an education are enemies of the race.

Implications

There are many factors that contribute to the educational achievement gap between blacks and whites on the collegiate level from within and outside of the black race. However, the influences outside of the African-American race will be the concentration of this section. In conjecture, the influences outside of the African-

American race (BET and the Federal Communications) appear to serve as a two-edged sword to keep the African-American race suppressed. BET serves as a blindfold over the eyes of African-Americans to education, while the Federal Communications Commission are the hands that tied the knot. By the Federal Communications Commission allowing African-American Hip-Hop artists to produce music about the benefits of selling drugs, to express their willingness to kill other African-Americans, to disparage them as "niggers," "bitches," and "hoes," to encourage rebellion against the law, and produce children out of wedlock; rather than promoting education, the FCC's lack of oversight gives permission to people of other races to exploit African-Americans in the same manner.

Limitations

The limitations of this research were time and lack of statistical data pertaining to college degree possession of athletes and inmates. I was only allotted six-weeks to assemble and process the data for this research article. Also, the National Football

League, the Arena Football League, Major League Soccer, and Major League Baseball professional sports organizations did not furnish me with the statistical data pertaining to the percentage of professional players without college degrees. The Federal Bureau of Prisons (an agency of the U.S Department of Justice) did not supply the statistical data pertaining to the percentage of inmates that possess college degrees. The Federal Bureau of Investigation and the Charlotte-Mecklenburg Police Department also did not provide the average revenue generated by lower and higher-level drug dealers.[3]

---

[3]Lower level drug-dealer=street drug-dealer; Higher level drug-dealer=Cartel status (has businesses and corporations involved in drug-trafficking)

References

Bailey, Benjamin. (2001). Dominican-American Ethnic/Racial Identities and United States Social Categories. *International Migration Review* 35 (3), 677-708.

Biblarz, T. J. & Raftery, A. E. (1999). Family Structure, Educational Attainment, and Socioeconomic Success: "Rethinking the Pathology of Matriarchy". *American Journal of Sociology*, 105(2), 321-365.

Black Entertainment Television. (2006, July). BET All Shows List. Retrieved July 18, 2006 from www.bet.com/BETShows/

Boost Mobile. (2006). About Boost Mobile: Why Boost is different (Advertising). Retrieved July 19, 2006 from www.boostmobile.com

Cable News Network. (CNN). (2004). *FCC preparing to hit Stern again.* Retrieved June 2006, from http://money.cnn.com/2004/04/05/news/fortune500/stern_fines/

Cable News Network. (CNN). (2004) *Clear Channel Nixes Howard Stern.* Retrieved June, 2006, from http://money.cnn.com/2004/04/08/news/fortune500/stern_fines/

Cohen, Sandy. (2006, June). Foxx, Blige, Brown, T.I. Among BET Winners. Boston Globe: A&E. Retrieved July 19, 2006 from www.boston.com

Dodoo, F. N. (1997) Assimilation Differences Between Africans in America. *Social Forces, 76*(2), 527-546.

Phi Delta Kappan. (1980). Why do some Urban Schools Succeed? The PDK Study of Exceptional Urban Elementary Schools. Study Summary Retrieved July 18, 2006, from www.pdkmembers.org. Duckett, R. Williard, Park, L. Don, & Clark, L. David.

Dunlap, E., Golub, A., & Johnson, B. D. (2006). The Severely-Distressed African American Family in the Crack Era: Empowerment is not Enough. *Journal of Sociology and Social Welfare,* 33(1).

Public/Private Ventures. (2001). *Challenges and Opportunities in After School Programs*. Philadelphia, PA Grossman, Baldwin Sean, Walker, Karen, & Raley Rebecca.

Journal of Blacks in Higher Education. (2005). *Holding a Four-Year College Degree Brings Blacks Close to Economic Parity With Whites*. (News & Views 1-4). Retrieved June, 2006, from

http://www.jbhe.com/news_views/47_four-year_collegedegrees.html

Meeks, K. (2005). Bridging the Educational Divide. *Black Enterprise*, *36*(1), 148.

Moushey, B. (1996). *Protected Witness*. Retrieved June, 2006, from http://www.fear.org/carlos1.html

Murphy, S., Waldorf, D., & Reinarman, C. (1990). Drifting into Dealing: Becoming a Cocaine Seller. *Qualitative Sociology*, *13*(4), 321-343.

MSNBC. (2006). *FCC proposes $3.6 mil fine for CBS orgy scene.* Retrieved June 2006, from http://www.msnbc.msn.com/id/11844455/

National Basketball Players Association. *NBPA History.* Retrieved June 19, 2006, from www.nbpa.com/history.php%20

New York Times. (1992). *Howard Stern Is the Object Of F.C.C.* Retrieved June 2006, from http://select.nytimes.com/gst/abstract.html?

Office of Juvenile Justice. (2006). *Mission Statement.* Retrieved July 17, 2006 from http://ojjdp.ncjrs.org/about/missionstatement.html

Ogbu, J. (1978). *Minority Education and Caste: The American System in Cross Cultural Perspective*: Academic Press.

Perna, L. W. & Titus, M. A. (2005). The Relationship between Parental Involvement as Social Capital and College Enrollment: An Examination of Racial/Ethnic Group Differences. *The Journal of Higher Education, 76(5).*

Puzzanchera, C., Finnegan, T., & Kang, W. (2006). *Easy Access to Juvenile Populations Online*. Retrieved July 18, 2006 from www.ojjdp.ncjrs.org

Trotman, F. (2001). Involving the African-American Parent: Recommendations to increase the level of parent involvement within African-American families. *The Journal of Negro Education (JSTOR)*, *70*(4), 276-277.

TV.com, (2006). Search Results*: 106 & Park, Rap City, and College Hill*. Retrieved July 18, 2006 from www.TV.com

United Nations. (1997). *Protection among Youth of the Ideals of Peace, Mutual Respect and Understanding between Peoples*. New York, New York: Office of the United Nations High Commissioner for Human Rights.

United Nations. (1997). *Convention on the Prevention and Punishment of the Crime of Genocide*. New York, New York: Office of the United Nations High Commissioner for Human Rights.

U.S. Census Bureau. (2005). *Parent and Family Involvement in Education.* Washington, DC: National Center for Education Statistics, 132-182.

U.S. Census Bureau. (2004). *Percentage of High School Dropouts.* Washington, DC: National Center for Education Statistics.

U.S. Census Bureau. (2006). *Percentage of High School Dropouts.* Washington, DC: National Center for Education Statistics.

U.S. Census Bureau. (2006). *The Condition of Education in Brief.* Washington, DC: National Center for Education Statistics.

U.S. Census Bureau. (1999). *Crosscutting Statistics Educational Attainment., Education Statistics Quarterly, 2*(3). Washington, DC: National Center for Education Statistics.

U.S. Census Bureau. (2004). *Children and the Households They Live In (2000)*, Census Special Reports. Washington, DC

U.S. *Department of Justice. (2006). Prison and Jail Inmates at midyear 2005.* Washington, DC: *Bureau of Justice Statistics.*

U.S. Department of Justice. (2005). *Prison and Jail Inmates 2004.*

Washington, DC: *Bureau of Justice Statistics.*

U.S Census Bureau. (2004). *Annual Demographic Survey, March Supplement, Annual Demographic Survey CPS 2005 Annual Social and Economic Supplement* 1-2. Washington, DC

USA Funds. (2004). *USA Funds Educational Access: African-American-Student Retention Involves Unique Challenges.* Retrieved June 6, 2006, from http://www.usafund.org/news/27jan2004/dmp012704a.htm

Verducci, T. (2003). Blackout: The African-American baseball player is vanishing. Does he have a future? *Sports Illustrated.* Retrieved June, 2006 from http://sportsillustrated.cnn.com/si_online/news/2003/07/10/black _ballplayer/

In Search of an Identity:
Black Religion, Philosophy, and Christ

2011

Identity is important. It is fundamental to the healthy existence of human beings. It provides the foundation for an understanding of self as well as for personal connection to others. In knowing themselves, individuals and groups are better able to engage with others with whom they share a common bond through similar behaviors, values, traditions, and beliefs (Stuart & Jose 1817-1819). Through these points of connection, individuals can more fully understand the world in which they live, and concurrently take pride in their individuality (Williams & Takahashi 1). Out of this same framework for identity derives ethnic identity, which is formed by shared culture, language, religion, and geography of people who are often united by a strong sense of loyalty kinship and nearness of location (Stuart & Jose 1817-1819).

Since slavery, we as Blacks, our original identities flattened, erased, and largely lost, have been searching to unearth and reclaim our identity; in our earnest search, we have accordingly developed religions, philosophies, and ideologies along the way. The search perhaps reached its peak between 1896 and 1964. Inspired by the Marcus Garvey movement from 1914-1927, Black leaders founded other faiths to counter the influence of Christianity in the Black community, as many of them viewed Christianity as the religion of the racist white man. As a result, Blacks, especially those in the Northern United States, were presented with a variety of religious identities, which in reality served as new or proxy systems through which to explain and confirm Black racial identity. The religions they founded ranged from new iterations of Islam to Black Judaism. And, although Christianity remained the primary faith of Black Americans during these early decades of the 20th century, no small number of Blacks opted for the alternative religions.

Many Blacks saw these faiths outside of Christianity as having the ability to address their socio-economic problems, particularly when such faiths assumed ethnocentric doctrines. Some Blacks felt more inclined to join faiths other than Christianity, especially since Christianity was seen as a religion that would have its followers receive freedom only in the afterlife. The founders of these new faiths developed many elaborate mythologies to attract followers, all the while alleging that theirs was the only way to salvation. These religions were very exclusive, promising Black salvation for Black people, claiming supremacy over the other ethnic groups. Not surprisingly, many of them also promised retribution of their God on the White race for its crimes against the Negro with their punishment always being either utter destruction or enslavement to Blacks.

The thought of God's repaying the White man Himself was a novel concept in a society where the Christian God was supposedly White and the Messiah was represented as blonde-haired, blue-eyed, and caring nothing for Blacks. It is this doctrine of Black supremacy that appealed to many African-Americans, especially to the poor, amongst whom these religions had their start. It provided them with a sense of hope and value amidst a condition of despair and degradation. Throughout the 20th century and even to the present, various strains of anti-Christian, ethnocentric Black religiosity in the United States have endured. Despite this problem, not enough has been done to address the accusations that these Black religions make against Christianity, to challenge the validity or authenticity of their claims to being of divine origin, or to challenge the explanations for the purpose of Black slavery which is advanced by these others faiths. Moreover, the Black Christian explanation for African-American slavery, old as such an explanation is, has often fallen by the wayside. By not addressing the issue of American slavery from a Biblical perspective, Black Christians have endured a seemingly endless cycle of misunderstanding as to their collective purpose in the world. This chapter will attempt to satisfy those concerns by attending to the following questions: What was, or possibly ever could have been, God's purpose for slavery? Are the aforementioned alternative religions of divine origin? Is Christ of Divine origin? What is, or ought to be the faith of the Black man? To understand why Blacks identify with Christ at all, He must be taken from the lens of ethnic misconceptions and portrayed accurately from a historical, Biblical, philosophical, and supernatural lens. In this multifaceted way, one will be able to perceive better His superiority.

God's Purpose for Slavery

"You intended to harm me, but God intended it for good to accomplish what is now being done, the saving of many lives." Genesis 50:20 (New International Version-NIV)

The idea of a divine purpose for suffering in general, and slavery, in particular, is neither new nor unique. In the Holy Bible, we are clearly told by Joseph that God had a divine plan for his suffering, stating to his brothers, "As for you, you meant evil against me, but God meant it for good in order to bring about this present result, to preserve many people alive" (Gen. 50:20 New American Standard Bible-NASB). Knowing this, one may then ask: Why, in fact, did God allow slavery? This question left unasked, in the American context, could cause ongoing bitterness toward Whites and resentment toward God. If left unanswered, it could cause ongoing anger at our present condition—the disadvantaged state of Blacks, and conversely, White people's seemingly perpetual profit from the vile injustices of slavery. This question is especially central to the issue of Black American identity. To misunderstand God's providence in this matter is to misunderstand the core purpose of the African-American experience. And it is because of numerous misinterpretations of God's will concerning African-American slavery that the alternative Black religions were formed. Therefore, an attempt to explain God's purpose will be made through a review of certain historical, Biblical, and economical truths.

First, to begin to understand God's purpose for slavery, we need a historical point of reference. The only group of people in the world that African-Americans share such close historical commonalities in suffering with is Israel. Jews were, of course, slaves in Egypt for 430 years; we, as Blacks, were enslaved persons in the United States for 250 years and abroad for nearly 400 years (Exod. 12:40, NIV; Hines et al. 30, 57, 289). Both ethnic groups were built through slavery. Nearly everywhere the Jewish people set foot, they were discriminated against; and everywhere Blacks were sent as slaves, they have been discriminated against. With such closeness in experience, it is safe to apply God's purpose for allowing them to be enslaved, to the reason for our enslavement, as well as the promises made by God that would follow.

Mankind is predisposed to cruelty. God, however, is not cruel to us. Slavery was not a punishment from God, for the nation of Israel was enslaved for 430 years with this promise to Jacob (Israel) their forefather, "… I will make you into a great nation there" (Gen. 46:3 NASB). Just as Joseph's initially troubled story ultimately served to glorify God, God's purpose for Blacks and Jews was arguably to build up a people, not destroy them.

Furthermore, not only did God promise that He would make His people into a great nation, but He also promised that He would provide them a homeland (Gen. 46:4 NASB). We often equate the suffering of American slavery with God's punishment, but it might rather be seen as the megaphone of God to rally us to Himself. Interestingly, this position has been argued by Black American preachers and theologians for centuries. They asserted that such suffering, was in fact, necessary for the construction of us as a people. For "… sympathy is not achievable without misery, or patience without tribulation. Courage is unobtainable without fear, and endurance is occasioned only by hardship" (Geisler & Bucchino 239). That said, what followed soon after the Hebrew nation's captivity was a meeting with the living God and an introduction to holiness that would set them apart from every other nation on earth (Exod. 19-20 NASB). This too, applies to us, who have been introduced to holiness in Christ through our captivity.

Not only is this assertion valid comparatively, but it also appears sound because in West Africa, "… all tribal groups [already] believed in a Supreme Creator of the world and [also] in an array of lesser gods tied to specific natural forces such as rain, fertility, and animal life" (Tindall & Shi 70). Now, through Christ, that Supreme Creator is no longer worshipped in ignorance, but with full identification. For had they known Him, they would have known, as Paul said to the Athenians,

> The God [the Supreme Creator] who made the world and everything in it is the Lord of heaven and earth … From one man he made every nation of men…and determined the

times set for them and the exact places where they should live. God did this so that man would seek him and perhaps reach out for him, though he not far from each one of us. 'For in him we live and *move* and have our being.' As some of your own poets have said, 'We are his offspring.' Therefore, since we are God's offspring, we should not think the divine being is like gold or silver or stone or image made by man's design or skill. In the *past* God overlooked such ignorance, but now he commands *all people everywhere* to repent. For he has set a day when he will judge the world with justice by the *man* he has appointed. He has given proof of this to all men by raising him from the dead. (Acts 17:22-24, 26-31 NIV, emphasis added)

Although we know only in part, and none of us is able in our limited understanding, to comprehend the totality of His divine will, it can still be argued theologically that God's purpose in allowing slavery was not to punish us, but to liberate us from that which kept us from having a relationship with Him through Christ. His aim was to build a new nation of people out of the West African nations that would be strong enough to carry the message of Christ throughout all of Africa; with the point of entry for Black Missionaries being our identification with them as brothers and sisters through our shared ethnic and multi-national heritage. How can this be true? It can be so because African-American leaders of the past believed and acted on this same supposition. According to Albert J. Raboteau in his book "Canaan Land," in 1808 in one of the earliest surviving sermons, Absalom Jones, rector of St. Thomas African Episcopal Church in Philadelphia, took up this very question of God's purpose for slavery. Jones opined, "Perhaps it was God's plan … that the descendants of the slaves learn Christianity … in order that they might become messengers of it, to the land of their fathers (Raboteau 33). Black contemporaries of Absalom Jones also acted on this belief as Raboteau further writes,

> It would be a divinely appointed task of African Americans
> to take the gospel of Christianity to Africa. David George, a

black Baptist minister, fled Savannah, Georgia, in 1782 with the departing British forces and went to Nova Scotia. There he preached to other black immigrants and founded a Baptist church. In 1792, he migrated again, this time with a colony of African Americans to Sierra Leone on the west coast of Africa, where he formed another Baptist church. Daniel Coker, a leader of the African Methodist Episcopal Church in Baltimore and one of the founding members of the denomination in 1816, sailed to Sierra Leone in 1820 to preach the gospel and to engage in trade. Lott Carey and Colin Teague, two members of the African Baptist Missionary Society of Richmond, Virginia, were sent as missionaries to Liberia in 1821. African-American churches lacked the resources to sponsor large-scale missions to Africa, but the ideal of Christianizing Africa held a great symbolic value for black Americans. The ideal provided them with a major role in the drama of world history: that God was drawing good out of the evil of slavery by using the American descendants of African slaves to take

Christianity back to the land of their ancestors. (Raboteau

33-34)

The idea that the institution of American slavery was God's

training regimen for African-Americans to lead future evangelistic

missions to Africa and the diaspora, upheld by former slaves and

their descendants during the period of the 1700s and 1800s, is still

a viable explanation for the "Maafa" or African-Holocaust that

remains a touchstone of African-American history today.

Philosophically, theologically, and teleologically the explanation is

even more relevant now in light of the fact that in centuries past,

Black missionaries worked with only menial resources to carry the

gospel to Africa, and yet accomplished great feats. How much

more responsible are we—a far wealthier and connected Black

nation—for sharing the word of Christ to our beloved Africa, as a

race of people whose buying power is projected to surpass 1.1

trillion by 2012 (Dodson 1)?

Searching for Identity 1896-1964

"For the time will come when men will not put up with sound doctrine. Instead, to suit their own desires, they will gather around a great number of teachers to say what their itching ears want to hear. They will turn their ears away from the truth and turn aside to myths." II Timothy 4:3-4 (NIV)

Between 1890 and 1930 over 2.5 million blacks migrated from the American South (Raboteau 82). Prompted by racial discrimination and the depressed economy, Blacks left the South for the expansion of industrial jobs in the North due to the onset of World War I in 1914 (83). It is from this "Great Migration" onward to 1964, that the presentation of alternative religious identities will be offered to counter Christianity in the Black community. To properly sequence the arrival of these religions, this period should be divided into two eras: before and after Marcus Garvey. This approach is necessary because the Garvey movement (1914-1927) significantly influenced those leaders who would follow him and institute alternative religions of their own.

Prior to the popularity of Marcus Garvey's ideology and philosophy among Blacks, some claimed they had discovered the true identity of Black people that had been erased during slavery (89). With the introduction of the Bible to enslaved Africans, Black Americans naturally identified with the Biblical Israelites, and considered their suffering to be emblematic of their own (89). However, the first Black leader to take this identification literally was William S. Crowdy, who in 1896 founded the Church of God and Saints of Christ in Lawrence, Kansas (89). Crowdy preached to his followers that Black people were descendants of the ten lost tribes of Israel (89). Since the founding of this organization, the ideology of "The Black Jew/Hebrew" has flourished. Raboteau writes,

> Similar beliefs inspired the development of several black Jewish congregations in New York. In the 1920s, Wentworth A. Matthew formed the Commandment Keepers Congregation of the Living God, for years Harlem's largest congregation of black Jews. The Commandment Keepers believed that African Americans were "Ethiopian Hebrews" who had been robbed of their true religion by slavery.

Judaism was the ancestral heritage of the Ethiopians,

whereas Christianity was the religion of the "Gentiles," that

is whites. (89)

Wilson Jeremiah Moses in his work "African American Religious

Thought," and Michael Miller in "Black Judaism(s) and the

Hebrew Israelites" shed further light on the group, stating,

> "Black Jews" can be used as an umbrella term indicating
>
> the subset of Jews who are of (sub-Saharan) African
>
> descent . . . those Judaizing groups, African American in
>
> origin . . . take some aspects of Jewish practice and identity
>
> while not seeking incorporation into the main body of
>
> modern Judaism. These last are obviously [transitional]
>
> even in their status as Black Jews; they often reject any
>
> identification with the modern Jewish community or
>
> practice or at least are unwilling to undergo conversion,
>
> believing that would be relinquishing and submission of
>
> their own—allegedly longstanding—traditions and claim of
>
> identity to one that has no stronger such claim; sometimes

they perceive themselves or African Americans generally as the authentic descendants of the Israelites or Judaeans, while the people commonly known as Jews are seen as European interlopers who by some feat have become mistakenly regarded as linearly related to the people of the Bible. . . .

The Black Jews in the United States were first studied by Raymond Jones, who focused his attention on Bishop Plummer of Washington, D.C., organizer of the Church of God and Saints of Christ. The members of this group identified themselves as the "lost tribe of Israel," asserting that the Biblical Hebrews were originally black. Arther H. Fauset described a similar group in Philadelphia during the early forties. Under the leadership of Prophet Cherry, they were organized as the Church of God and known popularly as "Black Jews" or "Black Hebrews." This group was notable for its disdain of swine flesh, keeping of the Sabbath, opposition to all pictures or "graven images," tithing of its members, and contempt for Christianity, especially black storefront religion. The Church of God was open only to black people, the original inhabitants of the earth. The first white man was named Gehazi; he received his color as a result of a curse for sinfulness. This was an adaptation of the American Protestant myths identifying the origins of the black race with the curse of Cain or Noah's curse of Canaan.

[Now, the movement could be understood as divided into various sects]: the Pentecostal "Holiness Sects" of the early 20th century; the "Black Rabbinic" who adopt most of the normative Jewish practices while refusing conversion or integration into normative Judaism; the "Torah only Sects" who reject both rabbinic and New Testament texts; and the "Messianic Hebrews" who accept the messianic status of Jesus, while being essentially Judaizing in practice (i.e., they emphasize the Hebraic nature of Jesus' message and its particular or exclusive relevance to Israelites). (Moses

536; Miller 1-2)

After this ideology had its start in 1896, Marcus Garvey started gaining momentum through his massive, two-million-member Universal Negro Improvement Association (Raboteau 87). Founded in Jamaica in 1914, and New York two years later, this organization's sole purpose was to improve the condition of the Negro socially, politically, economically, culturally, and spiritually (87). Members of the UNIA, called "Garveyettes," met in buildings they styled "Liberty Halls," that provided jobs for the unemployed, soup kitchens, and temporary housing (87). They also sponsored various programs that included public meetings, concerts, dances, Sunday morning services, and afternoon Sunday schools (87). The UNIA also had its own national anthem, national flag, and steamship line (87). For those who felt estranged from the 'White practice' of Christianity, the UNIA held a weekly Sunday service consisting of hymnal reading, creed recitation, baptism rituals, a catechism, the image of Christ as a "Black Man of Sorrows" and the Virgin Mary as a "Black Madonna" (87). It also had two main slogans, "One God, One Aim, One Destiny" and "Up you mighty race" (89). These helped propagate the message of pride and unity among peoples of African ancestry (89). The UNIA, moreover, sponsored parades, with banners and full-dress uniforms, which promoted the ideals of Black identity and independence (89). To understand how Garvey's movement spread so rapidly in the Black community and what inspired the founders of the alternative religions that would follow, one must understand the history of Marcus Garvey.

Born in Jamaica, Marcus Garvey (1887-1940) was an activist and political thinker, and through the UNIA, he founded the first important Black Nationalist movement, a concept explored in depth later in the book (Rohmann 44-45). Garvey aimed to instill pride in Blacks' African heritage, encourage Black self-determination, and promote Black achievement. The flag he designed had red, black, and green bars to represent struggle, unity, and hope for the future (44-45). Similar to the thinking of Booker T. Washington, Garvey was skeptical about integration into a predominately White culture that was racist and callous to the aspirations of Black people (44-45). From his perspective, liberation from White prejudice and control was racial segregation and economic independence (44-45). He believed that modern African-Americans and Africans in the motherland were the descendants of the "chosen people" of the Bible, were morally and spiritually superior to the White race, but were oppressed and exiled for their sins (44-45). His "Back-to-Africa" program envisioned an end to colonialism in Africa and the opportunity for African-Americans and West Indian Blacks to return to their ancestral homeland (44-45). He encouraged Black business and set an example in the years following World War I by establishing several model corporations (44-45). One such corporation was the Black Star Line, which was intended to facilitate trade between Black businesses around the world (44-45). Garvey is known for regularly using religious terms in his rhetoric, and his members came to know him as "Black Moses," a messiah-type (Hines et. al 438). In its efforts to expand, the UNIA attempted to establish a settlement on the Cavalla River in southern Liberia (439). Garvey even petitioned the League of Nations to allow the UNIA to assume control of the former German colony of Tangaruyaka (modern Tanzania; 439). Despite his efforts to uplift the Black race, many Black leaders, as well the United States government, opposed him and sought his ouster from power (439). Regrettably for his followers, Garvey was arrested, indicted, and eventually deported on twelve counts of fraudulent use of U.S. mail to sell stock in the Black Star Line enterprise in 1922 (439-440). For the "crime," Garvey was sent to a federal penitentiary in Atlanta in 1925. After two years, President Calvin Coolidge commuted his sentence and Garvey was deported to Jamaica (440). The UNIA could not sustain itself after the loss of Marcus Garvey and slowly dissolved between the 1920s and '30s (440). In 1940, Marcus Garvey died in London, England (440). Despite his death, the ideology and philosophy of Marcus Garvey would live on and become a cornerstone of the Black nationalist, Black power, and Civil Rights movements of the mid-20th century (Rohmann 159).

As previously stated, the Marcus Garvey movement would greatly impact those Black leaders who would follow after his death, and institute alternative religions of their own. When reviewing the history and doctrine of the following religions, one can readily conclude that all of them have been inspired in whole or in part, by the philosophy of racial pride espoused by Marcus Garvey. Their doctrines include: hatred of the White race (reverse racism), replacement theology (the belief that the Jewish people as we know them today are not the Jews of Biblical times, and that their religious group are the true "chosen people" of God), the worship of men elevated to "god" status by their followers, and the use of Biblical terms (or supposed ones) such as "God's chosen people," "Zion," or "Jah" (although that is an incorrect translation of the name of Biblical God. It is properly pronounced, "Yah;" Strong et. al 1401, reference 3068). Although there are more, this section will only focus on the four major Black alternative religions: The Nation of Islam, The Nation of Gods and Earths, Black Judaism/Hebrewism, and Rastafarianism.

The Nation of Islam, also known as the "World Community of Al-Islam in the West," was founded in 1930 by Wallace D. Fard (Raboteau 90-91). He first gained a following by teaching poor blacks in Detroit that they were members of the Muslim "lost-found" tribe of Shabazz (90-91). He also taught that salvation for the Black race was found in having "knowledge of self" (90-91) In 1993, Fard was arrested for disturbing the peace, and ordered to leave Detroit (90-91). Before he left, Fard entrusted his followers to the care of his chief assistant, Elijah Poole (later renamed "Elijah Muhammed" by Fard), who would guide the movement for the next forty years (90-91). This organization, which Fard named "The Nation of Islam," started with two small congregations in Detroit and Chicago and grew to have numerous mosques with thousands of members in every area of the country (90-91). Elijah Muhammed taught his followers that "Master" Fard had been the actual incarnation of Allah and that he was his messenger (90-91). At the core of this "Black Islam" was a religious mysticism crafted to counter the doctrines of White supremacy which many followers were familiar with (Moses 539). Whites were viewed as a cursed race of devils brought into existence by the skillful cunning of the mad scientist, "Yakub" (539). They taught that the religion of the White man was Christianity, while the religion of the original Black people was Islam (539). From their perspective, Allah has allowed this cursed race of White devils to rule the world for 6000 years (539). Doomed by its sinfulness to oblivion, the White race was viewed as a group to be separated from, which was the goal of The Nation of Islam (Moses 539; Raboteau 91). Like the Black Jews, the Black Muslims viewed Christians with absolute contempt (Moses 539).

Splintering from The Nation of Islam was The Nation of Gods and Earths, also known as "The Five Percent Nation" or "Allah's Nation of Five Percenters" (Smith 58-59). Founded by former NOI member Clarence 13X in Harlem in 1964, the movement began when Clarence openly challenged the doctrine that Wallace Fard was God (58-59). Being that the Nation of Islam taught that the original Black man was God, and it was evident that

Fard was not Black, Clarence concluded that Fard could only be human (58-59). As a result, Clarence soon believed and taught that not only was God Black, but that by extension, all Blacks were God themselves (58-59). Following a reprimand by the Nation, Clarence 13X, along with some of his associates, left and began preaching to Black youth on the street (58-59). The Five Percenter doctrine is a complex amalgam of vague Islamic symbolism, Black supremacy theory, and popular culture (58-59). Further distinguishing himself from the NOI, Clarence added to the NOI teachings about the original Black man a classification of people based on percentages (58-59). The largest group is the eighty-five percent of the world's populous who do not know God, are incapable of salvation, and only work to destroy themselves and others (Smith 58-59). The next ten percent possess knowledge and power but are considered oppressors because they teach that God is a "Spook" (Ghost) who cannot be seen physically (58-59). This group includes virtually all religions that believe God is a Spirit, especially White Christians and orthodox Muslims (58-59). After the ten percent, comes the five percent who are considered the,

> [P]oor righteous teachers who do not believe in the
> teachings of the ten percent and are all-wise and know who
> the Living God is and teach that the Living God is the Son
> of Man, the Supreme Being, or the Black Man of Asia, and
> teach Freedom, Justice and Equality to all the human
> family of the planet Earth; otherwise known as civilized
> people, also as Muslims and Muslim Sons. (Bailey 171)

Five Percent ideology also incorporates Sufism—a type of

Islamic mysticism—that practices the science of interpreting the

meaning of letters in the Arabic Alphabet (58-59). From this

expression of Islam, the Five Percenters developed a sophisticated

system called the "Supreme Alphabet," which pairs the letters of

the English alphabet with concepts affirming Black divinity and

empowerment (Andrews 155). This science is balanced by another

system called the "Supreme Mathematics" that assigns moral

meanings to numbers zero through nine which helps governs how

members function in the world (Andrews 33; Smith 58-59). The

Supreme Mathematics also relates to similar interpretations in some parts of Islamic Sufism (Smith 58-59). Restricted only to the initiates,

> Five Percenters use the Supreme Alphabet and Supreme Mathematics to perform a type of gematria through which acolytes "break down" words and numbers to discover their esoteric meanings. This process is referred to as "doing science" and provides the basis for the Five Percenter practice of "building", a theological discussion which is the main source of public meaning making within the Five Percent. (Andrews 33)

Moreover, the Five Percenters elevate Black males to the status of Gods by teaching that their appropriate name is "Allah," which is an acronym for the physical members of the body: arm, leg, leg, arm, head (Smith 58-59). To reflect their divine status, Black men in this movement often take on names such as "God Allah Mind" or "Allah Supreme" (58-59). As mentioned earlier, this group is also known as the Nation of Gods and Earths. In this vein, men are considered, "Gods," and the women, "Earths," for their ability to bring forth life (58-59). In fact, the only way a woman of this faith can be a Muslim is if she testifies that her man is "Allah" (58-59). Being productive in life is stressed, as special emphasis is placed on bearing the child of "God" (58-59). This religion is primarily propagated through Hip-Hop music and is very popular among African-American youth (58-59). Popular Hip-Hop artists such as Rakim, Poor Righteous Teachers, Gangstarr, J-Live, Wu-Tang Clan, Brand Nubian, Planet Asia, Nas, and AZ all spread the Five Percent Nation theology (Smith 58-59; Andrews 138-141).

Another religion that takes more directly from Marcus Garvey is Rastafarianism. Rastafari has been described as a religion, a social movement, and a sub-culture (Salamone 70-77). Most devotees of Rastafari prefer to use the term, "livity" to describe their world and cultural practices in their entirety, arguing that Rastafarianism is a lifestyle founded upon theocratic principles (Salamone 70-77). Rastafarians declare that Emperor Haile Salassie

I of Ethiopia (1892-1975) is the living God, "Jah Rastafari" (Salamone 70-77). They worship him under the name he used before being crowned Emperor, Ras (Prince) Tafari (Salamone 70-77). Rastafarians further assert that under his divine leadership, Africans whose ancestors were taken from Africa against their will to be enslaved in "Babylon" (the oppressive Western society) have the right of return to Africa (Salamone 70-77). According to their faith, Africa as a whole, and Ethiopia specifically, are "Zion," thought to be the true home of all blacks and the source of life, civilization, and redemptive power (Salamone 70-77). This mystical heaven they contrast with Babylon, which they describe as the post-colonial diaspora of Western society, and the White power establishment that throughout history has oppressed, enslaved and brutalized peoples of African descent (Salamone 70-77). Also, according to Rastafari, Black people are the reincarnated Israelites of the Bible who have been subjugated by the evil and inferior White race as divine punishment for their sins (Salamone 70-77). However, they believe they will finally experience redemption by returning to Africa, and will one day force the White man to be their servant (Encyclopedia of World Religions).

Nearly all of these religions conferred on their initiates an identity of hatred, superiority, and racial pride through their teaching of Black divinity, Black supremacy, and Black identity theft of the Jewish people. Therefore, it is no coincidence that these religions arose between 1890 and 1964, when the condition of the Black race in America was desperate and near hopeless. In 1896, the Supreme Court ruling on the Plessy v. Ferguson case instituted the "separate but equal" doctrine (Jim Crow segregation), which held that Blacks and Whites were to be segregated in all public facilities, public accommodations, housing, education, medical care, and employment with the caveat that they be of equal quality for Whites and Blacks. However, it is unmistakable that its actual purpose was to "… offer clear and undeniable that African-Americans would be required by law to regard themselves as second-class citizens—forever" (Duncan 79). Having its most profound impact in the South, Blacks throughout this region were subjected to,

> Southern whites [who were] determined to use both the law and extralegal intimidation to restore their domination … by establishing a rigid economic, political, and social caste system. By 1900, southern blacks had been effectively denied the right to vote, reduced to a condition of quasi serfdom in most rural areas, and … a system of legally mandated segregation that barred social interaction between whites and blacks in almost every area of life, including education. (Hartman et al. 35)

In the North, Blacks did not fare much better. In his book, "Sweet Land of Liberty: The Forgotten Struggle for Civil Rights in the North" Thomas J. Sugrue writes,

> In the 1920s, blacks faced growing hostility in the North. Throughout the region, restrictive covenants—clauses in home deeds that forbade blacks and other minorities from purchasing or renting homes—proliferated. Nearly every new housing development built during the booming 1920s

was closed to blacks. Those who attempted to breach the invisible color lines that separated neighborhoods faced violent reprisals. The result was a steep rise in housing segregation. The Ku Klux Klan gained strongholds in nearly every northern city in the 1920s. Chicago's Klan, for example, had nearly forty thousand members, and nearly one in three white men in Indiana belonged to the group at its peak in the mid-1920s. In Detroit, a Klansman lost election to the Detroit mayoralty on a technicality in 1924. Blacks faced growing restrictions. Shopkeepers, restaurant owners, and theater managers, proclaimed their premises for whites only. And racially separate schools proliferated, particularly in northern towns that attracted large numbers of black migrants. Nearly all of these proscriptions—as Wilkins called them—were defended by law enforcement authorities. (6)

With the downtrodden state of the Black race during this period psychologically, socially, economically, and politically; it could only be expected that new religions and philosophies would arise in an attempt to reverse the African-American condition. Therefore, it should be understood that that the motivating factor behind the establishment of these religions was not of divine inspiration, but the natural response of Blacks to the racial discrimination they faced at the time.

The Abuse of Christ

"We also know that law is made not for the righteous but for lawbreakers and rebels, the ungodly and sinful, the unholy and irreligious…for the murderers, for adulterers and perverts, for slave traders and liars, and perjurers—and for whatever else is contrary to the sound doctrine that conforms to the glorious gospel of the blessed God…" I Timothy 1:9 (NIV)

Some may attempt to counter the conclusion of the previous chapter with this question: "Could not one say that Christianity was only the natural response of the Jewish people to the discrimination they faced at the time, since Christ came at a time when the Jewish people were oppressed by the Roman Empire?" The answer is, "No." For though the Jewish people were oppressed by the Roman Empire, Christ's message and mission were never about liberation from the Roman Empire and the establishment of a Jewish kingdom with him as their conquering King; but spiritual liberation from bondage to sin and the establishment of the kingdom of God, with Him as their lowly Savior (Isa. 53; Luke 4:18-19, 19:10 NIV).

His attitude was the opposite of what the Jewish populous had in mind for what the Messiah was supposed to accomplish— one of many reasons for their disbelief in His claim to being the

Messiah, and one reason for their demand that he be crucified.

Even the apostles envisioned a physical kingdom appearing

following the resurrection of Christ from the dead. The Bible says:

> So when they met together, they asked him, "Lord are you
>
> at this time going to restore the kingdom to Israel? He said
>
> to them, "It is not for you to know the times or dates the
>
> Father has set by his own authority. (Acts 1:7 NIV)

However, the scriptures make clear that Christ's attitude

was contrary to the establishment of an independent Jewish

kingdom. One example of Him rejecting this idea can be found in

his response to the five thousand men who wanted to make Him

king after He miraculously fed them. The Bible says,

> After the people saw the miraculous sign that Jesus did,
>
> they began to say, 'Surely this is the Prophet who is come
>
> into the world.' Jesus, knowing that they intended to come
>
> and make him king by force, withdrew again to a mountain
>
> by himself. (John 6:14-15 NIV)

Though Christianity is of divine origin, while the urban

Black religions are not, it should be understood, as previously demonstrated, that those religions were founded upon a history of African-American abuse in Christ's name. Although the abuse of the message of Christ dates back to the first century, the most significant abuse, as it relates to Blacks, began with American slavery from 1640-1865 (Hine et al. 57, 289). During this time, many slave owners either denied their slaves access to Christianity or would only teach "plantation Christianity." That is, the use of scripture to keep the enslaved Africans in bondage to their masters (154). Hine et al. writes, "In plantation churches, white ministers told their black congregations that Christian slaves must obey their earthly masters as they did God" (154).

In the late eighteenth century, those churches that would be so bold as to house Black and White in the same building, had racially segregated seating, communion services, Sunday schools, cemeteries, and denied Blacks significant influence in church governance (115). The outcome of such policies was that separate Black congregations that were usually led by Black ministers were made subject to White church hierarchies (115). During the

Revolutionary War, using such lofty ideals that can be traced to

Christ in the Declaration of Independence, slaveholders such as

Thomas Jefferson (who wrote the DOI) clamored for independence

from the oppressive British Empire (84). Blacks and anyone else

who applied only the simplest logic, could see the gross hypocrisy

of their actions (84). White Americans wanted freedom from

Britain but were unwilling to free their African-American slaves

(84). Also, the constitution which is popularly considered as having

been written under "divine inspiration," did not secure any rights

for African-Americans or women until the additions of the 13th,

14th, and 15th amendments from 1865-1870 (Appendix A-9).

Moreover, there were terrorist organizations claiming to be

acting in the name of the Lord. One of the most famous being the

Ku-Klux-Klan—a White supremacist, White nationalist

organization founded 1866 (Wade 31). Its first Grand Wizard was

the ruthless Confederate General, Nathan Bedford Forrest, who

was famous for his massacre of surrendered Black Union troops at

Fort Pillow during the Civil War (Wade 33, 40; Hine et. al 276).

The Klan maintained that all other ethnic groups were inferior to the White man and should be subjected to second-class citizenship (Wade 37, 47-49, 199). Since the beginning of its existence, the Klan has committed acts of violence, rape, arson, and terrorism against Blacks, other minority groups, and anyone who supported equal rights for minorities (37, 47-49, 199). However, despite these acts, the Klan was for generations esteemed as a Christian organization that was only concerned with doing the Lord's work in America. Their prestige as an organization reached its zenith during the period between 1922-1925 when Christian Fundamentalism merged with the Klan, resulting in nearly forty-thousand ministers becoming members (171). In numerous tracts, Klansmen avowed,

> We honor the Christ as the Klansmen's *Only Criterion of Character.* And we seek at His hands that cleansing from sin and impurity which only He can give. We believe that the highest expression of life is in service and in sacrifice

for that which is right; selfishness can have no place in a true Klansmen's life and character; but that he must be moved by unselfish motives, such as characterized our Lord the Christ and moved Him to the highest service and the supreme sacrifice for that which was right. (168-171)

Around the time the Klan was founded, "Christian Identity"—an off-shoot of "British Israelism"—a racist and anti-Semitic interpretation of Christianity, arose and became the ideological anchor for numerous other White supremacist /nationalist organizations. Established in the mid-nineteenth century by self-educated lecturer John Wilson, Christian Identity,

> Also known as British Israelism, Israel Identity, and Kingdom Message, the Christian Identity Movement . . . is comprised of a loose collection of congregations that share the belief that white Christians are the true "Israelites" of the Old Testament, and are therefore God's chosen people—contrary to traditional Christian teaching, which assigns this role to the Jews. According to Christian

Identity, the ten lost tribes of Israel were the actual

predecessors of Nordic, British and American whites;

modern-day Jews are descendants of a historically separate

kingdom of Judah. Great Britain became the modern-day

Israel after the lost-tribes traveled there via two great

migration routes. One path led through Spain, into Scotland

and Ireland, and from there to the current British ruling

family—who are, of course, Lost Israelites. Other tribes

populated the rest of the white world, including America,

which was settled by the Manasseh. The Manasseh was the

thirteenth tribe, and thirteen is a recurrent number in

American custom . . . thirteen original colonies, thirteen

stars and stripes on the flag. (Barkun 6-11; Ridgeway 71)

Tanya Sharpe in her work, "The Identity Christian Movement:

Ideology of Domestic Terrorism," concurs with Ridgeway,

asserting that,

Identity Christian believers have adopted a unique version

of the polygenist view of man's origin. Polygenists hold

that humanity had several distinct origins and is opposed to the belief that all mankind comes from one genetic source, for example, the biblical figure Adam . . . Although Identity Christians generally cling to literal interpretation of the Bible, they believe that Whites were created by God in his likeness and are the descendants of Adam and Eve. In contrast, they believe that all non-Whites evolved from pre-Adamic, lower species . . . Thus, they combine a creation origin for Whites with an evolutionist origin for non-Whites. In other words, Whites are the result of Divine creation and others are the result of evolution and are considered less-than-human, "mud people" (610).

Despite these abuses, Christ and His written word remain faultless. The unadulterated gospel of Christ makes no allowance for racism or prejudice—sins made permanent in America by the slave trade. The Bible says in I Tim. 1:9-11 (NIV),

"We also know that law is made not for the righteous but for lawbreakers and rebels, the ungodly and sinful, the unholy and irreligious . . . for the murderers, for adulterers and perverts, for *slave traders* and liars, and perjurers—and for whatever else is contrary to the sound doctrine that conforms to the glorious gospel of the blessed God . . ." (emphasis added)

All who participated in sustaining and expanding the slave trade embodied those attributes described in the above passage. Therefore, they could in *no way* be representative of Christ and were objects of His wrath. The Bible says,

1. Woe unto them that call evil good and good evil . . . (Isa. 5:20 King James Version-KJV)

2. Woe unto those who make unjust laws, to those who issue oppressive decrees, to deprive the poor of their rights and withhold justice from the oppressed . . . (Isa. 10:1 KJV)

3. Woe unto him who builds his palace by unrighteousness, his upper rooms by injustice, making his countrymen work for nothing, not paying them for their labor. (Jer. 22:13 KJV)

4. Woe to those who plan iniquity, to those who plot evil on their beds! At morning's light they carry it out because it is in their power to do it. They covet fields and seize them, and houses and take them. They defraud a man of his home, a fellow man of his inheritance. (Micah 2:1-2 KJV)

5. Woe to him who builds a city with bloodshed and establishes a town by crime. (Hab. 2:12 KJV)

6. Woe to him who builds his realm by unjust gain to set his nest on high, to escape the clutches of ruin! You have plotted the ruin of many peoples, shaming your own house and forfeiting your life. (Hab. 2:9-10 KJV)

Having demonstrated that the message of Christ is not the religion of the White slave master and did not justify the slave trade as the urban Black religions claim; it is now safe to analyze the doctrinal soundness of the urban Black religions in comparison to the faith of Christ.

The Supremacy of Christ

"The Lord has sworn and will not change his mind: 'You are a priest forever.'" Because of this oath, Jesus has become the guarantee of a better covenant." Hebrews 7:21-22 (NIV)

The supremacy of Christ to the urban Black religions is found in that His way of life, His teachings, and His plan of salvation, address not only the behavior, but also its source. The salvation of Christ promises a new, selfless, and loving nature as a replacement to the evil self-centeredness of the human nature. Thus, His ability reaches beyond the natural—making Him supernatural. We will discover this truth by analyzing the claims of the urban Black religions, and comparing them to the faith of Christ philosophically.

Nation of Islam:

The abbreviated philosophical arguments that will be made against the Nation of Islam will derive from the following three discussion points:

1. The NOI is a devolution of Orthodox Islam

2. The NOI argument that the original religion of Blacks was Islam.

3. The NOI argument that the white race is doomed by its own sinfulness but its own sin of hatred will go unpunished.

First argument: The NOI is a Devolution of Orthodox Islam

The Nation of Islam and its founder are not accepted by orthodox Muslims around the world (Braswell 83-84). Orthodox Islam asserts that Mohammed was the last prophet and that "Allah" never incarnated himself into anyone (13). There is also nothing ancient about the Nation of Islam—no ancient manuscripts, no eyewitnesses, or outside sources can verify that Wallace D. Fard was indeed "Allah incarnate." The NOI was founded less than a century ago in Detroit by Wallace D. Fard, teaching poor Blacks that they were members of the "lost-found" tribe of "Shabazz," and that salvation was through the "knowledge of self" (Raboteau 90). However, it makes no sense according to NOI theology for "Allah" to have chosen Fard as the vessel of his incarnation, since Fard was of a mixed heritage that was partly British according to the Detroit Police; and NOI doctrine classifies all White people as devils destined for destruction (Decaro 12; Moses 539). Therefore, Wallace D. Fard, according to NOI doctrine, is mixed with the devil. Which further implies that "Allah" chose to mix himself with the devil, and has doomed himself to utter destruction.

Second argument: The Original Religion of the Black Man was Islam

The assertion that the original religion of the Black man was Islam is unsound historically. Islam was not established until the middle of the 7th century A.D, and the continent of Africa was in existence thousands of years prior (Braswell 14). Therefore, it is impossible for the original religion of the Black man to be Islam. Additionally, Christianity was entrenched in North Africa centuries before the arrival of Islam (Speel 379).

Third argument: The White Race is Doomed to Oblivion Due to its Sinfulness

It is hypocritical to believe that "Allah" will punish the White race for the hatred they have shown Blacks but will condone the hatred of NOI members towards Whites and Black Christians.

It reveals the following about "Allah": 1. He is not a god of justice or equality. Rather, he is a double-minded deity, offering hope and paradise for Blacks and unalterable destruction for Whites. 2. He is not a god for all people but a particular group that subscribe to the teachings of NOI—which when reduced to its basic elements is hatred and Black supremacy. Any god that only offers hope to one ethnic group and not to the whole world is not god overall. Hence, he is no god at all.

The Black Hebrew Israelites/Black Jews

The arguments that will be made against the Black Hebrew Israelites will also derive from the following three discussion points,

1. The Black Hebrew Israelites/Black Jews have doctrinal beliefs similar to the Black Muslims.

2. Black Hebrew Israelites claim to be the descendants of the ancient Jewish people.

3. Black Hebrew Israelites restrict their membership to certain groups.

First argument: Their Commonalities with the Black Muslims

Doctrinally, the BHI and Black Muslims are virtually the same. They have a disdain for Whites, discount the Jewish people of Israel as the chosen people of God, and despise orthodox Christianity. The only difference is the Black Jews try to use the Bible to justify their religion, while the Black Muslims use the Koran. Therefore, there is nothing that sets the two apart and both can be counted as having originated from man.

Second argument: The Lineage Claim

BHI of African-American lineage claim to be the Jewish people of Biblical times. However, the father of the Jewish people was Abraham, and he did not originate from Africa but Ur of Chaldea, or the modern-day Iraq/Mesopotamia region. Individual African-Americans may have descended from African Jews but African-Americans as an ethnic group did not descend from African Jewry. Most African-Americans originate from West Africa (Lynch). There is also no need for the adoption of replacement theology by the Black Hebrew Israelites to secure

Black representation in the story of God. There are numerous

references to people of African descent having significant roles in

the Scriptures. The tribes of Ephraim and Manasseh were half-

African (Gen. 46:20 NASB); the Shulamite in Song of Solomon

was "dark" (Song of Sol.1:5-6 NASB); Simon of Cyrene (Libya)

who helped Christ carry the cross was African (Matt. 27:32

NASB); and two of the leaders in the Church at Antioch were of

African lineage: Simeon (also called, "Niger"— the Black man)

and Lucius of Cyrene (Acts 13:1 NASB). God also made specific

promises of salvation to peoples of African descent (Ps. 68:31;

Isa.19 NASB).

Third argument: Becoming a Citizen of Israel

The message of the Black Hebrew Israelites also contradicts

the citizenship process of Biblical Israel. Any stranger—with the

exception of the Ammonites and Moabites (Deut. 23:4 NASB)—

that wanted to become a citizen of Israel could do so as long as

they submitted to the covenant of Abraham and the law (Gen 17:1-

13; Exod. 12:49; Lev. 19:34; Isa. 56:2-7 NASB). With the BHI, only Blacks and some ethnic minorities are allowed to join.

Allah's Nation of Five Percenters

The arguments that will be made against the Five Percenters will also derive from the following four discussion points,

1. "Allah," the Black man, cannot bring salvation to all.

2. "Allah," does not teach salvation for all.

3. Five Percent doctrine steals from Orthodox Islam, yet condemns it.

4. Fiver Percent doctrine claims that God is not a "Spook" but they practice mysticism.

First argument: "Allah" Cannot Bring Salvation to All

According to the Five Percent Nation, 85 percent of individuals on earth are incapable of being saved. If so, then it is clear that the Black man ("Allah") could not be "God," because he is not able to save them. God is a supernatural being with power to control the universe.

Second argument: "Allah" Does not Teach Salvation for All

The five percent of righteous teachers are those who supposedly teach freedom, justice, and equality. But what is the purpose of teaching these principles when 85 percent of the world has no hope that "Allah" can provide? Where is the equality in this doctrine if in the Five Percent classification (caste) system, the Black man is placed at the top of the order and the rest of the world is beneath him?

Third argument: Five Percent Doctrine Steals from Orthodox Islam Yet Condemns it

How can this religion use terminology and dress that originated from Orthodox Islam and yet consider Islam to be a part of the oppressive 10 percent? The fact that this religion borrows from Orthodox Islam while simultaneously condemning it, makes arguments for their faith self-defeating, and their ministers hypocritical.

Fourth argument: Their Doctrine is Really the "Spook"

The Five Percent doctrine strongly denounces any faith that

teaches that God "cannot be physically seen" or is a "spook." However, if "Allah" of the Five Percent Nation is the Black man, and yet the Black man does not have the power to save 85 percent of the world, could it not be considered that the teaching of this "Allah" and his power is nothing more than a poorly written fairy tale?

The Supremacy of Christ

Contrary to the impotency of the Black cults, in Christ, one finds the greatest need of a man addressed—the need for reconciliation. Through faith in Christ, the strain of self-alienation, alienation from our fellow man, and alienation from nature all come to an end in Christ, as he reconciles us to God, and imparts life to every aspect of our lives. A lost people, with no direction, have need only to come to God through Christ to get victory over sin, move beyond the historical, spiritual, and psychological burdens of race and enter into the purpose for which God created them. Unfortunately, for too long, Blacks have been looking at the purpose of their experience in the Americas through a worldly lens, searching for other saviors, and so have remained wanderers—lost in a wilderness of their ideologies (ex. Black Nationalism, Pan-Africanism, Black Power, Afro-Marxism and etc.). But through faith in Christ, and careful observation and adherence to His ways, the path forward will become clear. Therefore, in this section, the reader will learn how Christ is superior to the Black cults and how Yeshua (Jesus) is the Savior for the Black man. We will work to accomplish this task using the following four arguments,

1. Christ died on the cross to validate his claim as Savior

2. The Black cults teach that the Black man must have "knowledge of self." Christ requires humanity to know Him.

3. Christ addressed the spiritual condition of man while the former religions only address the material conditions of the Black man.

4. Christ claimed to be the Savior for all men while the Black cults claim only to be able to save the Black man through their knowledge.

First Argument: Christ Died on the Cross to Validate His Claim as Savior

Christ died on the cross for His followers to validate His

claim as Savior while is not true of any of the Black Cultic leaders. Instead of feeding on the sheep, as is the case with countless leaders throughout history, Christ came so the sheep could feed on Him (John 6 NASB). He gave his life willingly to confirm that his mission was from God. When it was time for Him to die for the sins of the world, Roman soldiers scourged Christ severely, ripped out His beard and crucified Him, all while allowing Him to be mocked and spat upon (Isa. 50:5-6 NASB), The cross was the method of capital punishment by Rome, from which derives the term 'excruciating,' which literally means, "from the cross" (Driscoll and Breshears 18).

Second Argument: The Black Cults Say that Blacks Must Know who *they* are; Christ says Blacks must Know who *He* is.

How can a people cause supernatural change to take place within by hoping in themselves through knowledge? That can be considered a, "Do it yourself" approach where one must save themselves. If man cannot save himself from the natural inclination to do evil when he *knows* right from wrong, how can he save himself by so-called "knowledge of self" regardless of his identification with the "true Jews," or members of the "lost-found tribe of Shabazz," or are "Allah" (arm, leg, leg, arm, head)? Simply put, supernatural change requires Divine intervention. Knowledge alone is not enough. Christ said,

> If you love me, you will obey what I command. And I will ask the Father, and he will give you another Counselor to be with you forever—the Spirit of truth . . . he lives with you and will be in you. But when he, the Spirit of truth comes, he will guide you into all truth . . . he will tell you what is to come . . . He will bring glory to me . . . (John 14:16-17, 16:13-14 NIV)

When one accepts Christ as Savior, God not only forgives their sins and reconciles them to Himself, He also takes up residence inside and sustains them in His righteousness. The Scripture says, ". . . he will guide you into all truth . . ." (John 16:13 NIV). Meaning, He will lead the believer into all that is right, and guide them away from all that is evil so they can choose the good and reject the evil. Also, ". . . he will tell you what is to come . . . [and] . . . bring glory to [Christ]" (John 16:13-14 NIV). Only through the righteousness of God dwelling inside can the Christian bring glory to God. And what better way is there for a man to practice holiness and righteousness than for God Himself to be expressing it through him?

Third Argument: Christ Addressed the Spiritual Condition of Man, While the Black Cults Only Address the Physical.

The supremacy of Christ is found in His understanding that before any negative physical circumstances can change for the good, the heart of man that caused the condition must be changed first. If physical circumstances improve but the heart does not change, the circumstances will eventually revert. For this reason, the Bible says, ". . . if anyone be in Christ, he is a new creation; the old has gone, the new has come!" (II Corinthians 5:17 NIV) With the mind of Christ, the Christian's new attitude is: ". . . as we have opportunity, let us do good to all people . . . Love your enemies, do good to those who hate you, bless those who curse you, pray for those who mistreat you" (Galatians 6:10; Luke 6:27 NIV). It is this mindset that overcomes the forces of oppression, injustice, and evil. For, evil can never be defeated by another act of evil, as human vengeance only creates twice as much evil as before. No. Evil must be defeated by good, and that is the determination that Christ creates in the heart of the believer.

Fourth Argument: Christ claimed to be the Savior for All Men While the Former Religions Claim Only to be able to Save the Black Race through their Knowledge.

Christ said, "I am the light of the world. Whoever follows me will never walk in darkness, but will have the light of life" (John 8:12 NIV). To have the power to be the light of the world is greater than that of having the pretended power to be the light of a single ethnic group. If Yeshua has the power to be the light of the world, then He is also able to demonstrate greater power in any single ethnic group than they could ever produce on their own.

References

Andrews, Pamela. *Ain't No Spook God: Religiosity in the Nation of Gods and Earths.* Memorial University of Newfoundland, 2013, pp. 33, 138-141, 155.

Barkun, Michael. Religion and the Racist Right: The Origins of the Christian Identity Movement. University of North Carolina Press, 2014, p. 6-11.

Bonn, Gregory. "Primary Process Emotion, Identity, and Culture: Cultural Identification's Roots in Basic Motivation." *Frontiers in Psychology*, vol. 6, 2015, p. 1. *Crossref,* doi:10.3389/fpsyg.2015.00218.

Braswell, George. *Islam and America: Answers to the 31 Most-Asked Questions.* Broadman & Holman Publishers, 2005, pp. 13-14, 83-84.

Decaro, Louis A. *Malcolm and the Cross: The Nation of Islam, Malcolm X, and Christianity.* New York University, 1998, p. 12

Dobson, David. Minority Groups' Share of $10 Trillion U.S. Consumer Market Is Growing Steadily, According to

Annual Buying Power Study from Terry College's Selig
Center for Economic Growth. Terry College of Business,
2007, https://news.uga.edu/study-shows-minority-groups-
share-of-10-trillion-u-s-consumer-market-is-gr/.

Duncan, Melba. *The Complete Idiot's Guide to African-American
History*. Penguin Group, 2003, p. 79.

Driscoll, Mark, Breshears, Gerry. *Death by Love: Letters from the
Cross*. Goodnews Publishers, 2008, p. 18.

Encyclopedia of World Religions. Mirriam-Webster, 1999.

Geisler, Norman, and Bucchino, Peter. *Unshakable Foundations*.
Bethany House Publishers, 2001, p 239.

Hartman, Gary, et al. *Landmark Supreme Court Cases*. Facts on
File Inc., 2004, p. 35.

Hine, Darlene Clark, et al. *The African-American Odyssey*. Third
edition, Pearson Education, 2006, pp. 30, 57, 84 115, 154,
276 289, 438-440, Appendix A-9.

Jackson, Jennifer V., and Cothran Mary E. "Black versus Black:
The Relationship Among African, African American, and

African Caribbean Persons." *Journal of Black Studies*, vol. 33, no. 5, 2003, p. 578. Sage Publications, Inc.

Lynch, Hollis. "African Americans." *Encyclopedia Britannica*, 2020. https://www.britannica.com/topic/African-American.

Miller, Michael T. "Black Judaism(s) and the Hebrew Israelites. *Religion Compass*, 2019, pp. 1-2. *Wiley*, https://doi.org/10.1111/rec3.12346.

Moses, Wilson J. "Chosen Peoples of the Metropolis: Black Muslims, Black Jews, and Others." *African American Religious Thought: An Anthology*, edited by Cornel West and Eddie S. Glaude Jr., Westminster John Knox Press, 2003, p. 536.

Raboteau, Albert J., *Canaan Land: A Religious History of African-Americans*. OUP, 2001, pp. 33-34, 82-83, 87, 89, 90-91.

Ridgeway, James. *Blood in the Face.* Thunder's Mouth Press, 1995, p. 71.

Rohmann, Chris. *A World of Ideas A Dictionary of Important Theories, Concepts, Beliefs, and Thinkers*. Ballantine Books, 1999, pp. 44-45, 159.

Salamone, Frank A. *Encyclopedia of Religious Rites, Rituals, and Festivals*. Routledge, 2004, pp. 70-77.

Sharpe, Tanya T. "The Identity Christian Movement: Ideology of Domestic Terrorism." *Journal of Black Studies*, vol. 30, no. 4, 2000, p. 610. *JSTOR*, www.jstor.org/stable/2645906.

Smith, Jane I. *Islam in America*. Columbia University Press, 1999, pp. 58-59.

Speel, C. J. "The Disappearance of Christianity from North Africa in the Wake of the Rise of Islam." *Church History*, vol. 29, no. 4, 1960, p. 379. *JSTOR*, www.jstor.org/stable/3161925.

Strong, James, et al. *The Strongest Strong's Exhaustive Concordance of the Bible*. Zondervan, 2001.

Stuart, Jaimee and Jose, Paul E. "The Protective Influence of Family Connectedness, Ethnic Identity, and Ethnic Engagement for New Zealand Māori Adolescents."

Developmental Psychology, vol. 50, no. 6, 2014, pp. 1817–26. *Crossref*, doi:10.1037/a0036386.

Sugrue, Thomas J. *Sweet Land of Liberty: The Forgotten Struggle for Civil Rights in the North*. Random House, p. 6.

The Holy Bible: New International Version. The Zondervan Corporation, 1996.

The King James Bible. Edited by Frank Charles Thompson, B.B. Kirkbride Bible Company, Inc., 1988.

The New American Standard Bible. The Lockman Foundation, 1997.

Tindall, George, and David Shi. *America: A Narrative History*. 6th ed., W. W. Norton and Company, 2004 p. 70.

Wade, Wyn C. *The Fiery Cross*. Oxford University Press, 1987, pp. 31, 33, 37, 40, 47-49, 168-171, 199.

William Whiston, translators. *The Works of Josephus*. Hendrickson Publishers, 1987, Book 1, Chaps. 7, 38.

A Creed for Afro-Christian Self-Help

1. We will stop making White Americans the standard by which we measure successful living and start making Christ the standard by which we live.

2. We will stop chasing the American Dream and start pursuing God's plan for our lives.

3. We will stop striving to assimilate into White America and be assimilated into Christ—heart and soul.

4. We will stop comparing our spiritual, social, political, academic and economic progress to that of White Americans and be content with the gains we make year to year.

www.ingramcontent.com/pod-product-compliance
Lightning Source LLC
Chambersburg PA
CBHW061243120726
48001CB00001B/119